ENGLISH RUGBY: A CELEBRATION

ACKNOWLEDGMENTS

First and foremost, thanks are due to John Mason and John Reason, the leading Rugby Union writers of the *Telegraph* group, for their initial advice and subsequent contributions. Bob Thomas and his staff, particularly David Rogers, made picture hunting easy, and Tony Henshaw at Professional Sport, Joe Mann, David Shopland, the Press Association and Sport and General all made special camera contributions.

Thumbnail sketches of the contributors are given as an appendix and finally, thanks to George Chick, a junior club stalwart if ever there was one, for his invaluable practical help and suggestions.

UNDERWOOD RACES AWAY FROM SCOTLAND'S STANGER AT MURRAYFIELD IN THE WORLD
CUP SEMI-FINALS, 26 OCTOBER 1991 – BUT WAS CROWDED OUT ALMOST ON THE LINE

CONTENTS

PREFACE

186 – 44 – 146 / 11 – 1 – 31 / 197 – 45 – 177

Any merit possessed by this book is entirely the product of the knowledge and love of Rugby Union displayed by its contributors, a mix of distinguished players, coaches, administrators and writers – all four in some cases.

Rugby Union, it can be stated without exaggeration, has achieved more fundamental changes in England in the past decade than any other major sport (unbelievers read Terry Cooper on The Leagues). Radical surgery was not permitted without loud misgivings: yet in next to no time traditional ways and, in particular, hallowed and fiercely defended fixture lists have been abandoned with scarcely a backward glance. Perhaps even more surprisingly, the concept of status being dependent on open competition has been accepted with unlooked for enthusiasm.

These changes, along with determined efforts to give a unity and purpose to coaching and to rationalise national and club finances, may have had something to do with the awakening in recent seasons of what many observers, at home and abroad, looked upon as a sleeping giant, the England XV.

The 15 profiles of outstanding England players that appear hereunder are not intended to make up the best England XV of all time, but to give an indication of the many splendid talents England have used, or – as some of our writers suggest – misused, over the past few decades.

The figures that head these remarks represent England's won, drawn and lost account over 120 years of competition up to the end of the 1991 World Cup against, first, their Five Nations opponents, second, their southern hemisphere experiences at home and away, and third, England's overall record against the seven major Test-playing nations. This book contains several explanations of why that record is not better, considering the vast number of players available and that the sport is indisputably an English invention. Celebrations were in order. The 1980s had begun with a bang and continued with a good many whimpers, but they ended in a continuing revival, as results in the Five Nations tournament moved towards the perfection of the Grand Slam year with pleasing symmetry: against Scotland, Ireland, Wales and France respectively, the progression was: 1988 – WWLL; 1989 – DWLW; 1990 – LWWW; 1991 – WWWW. This particular 'celebration' was not written exclusively by wearers of rose-tinted spectacles, however. Indeed, the opinions by contributors viewing England from the standpoint of their chief rivals north and south of the equator permit us 'To see ourselves as ithers see us . . .' – not always a pretty sight, but one which might 'Frae mony a blunder free us'. On the other hand, it is noteworthy that the views of both Willie John McBride, from the other side of the Irish Sea, and Don Cameron, from the other side of the world in New Zealand, reflect greater faith in the medium and long-term benefits that will accrue from the Courage League and allied reforms than do the judgments of some domestic die-hards. However, the game's leadership at Twickenham will not be surprised at this, since prophets seldom achieve much honour on their native turf.

Perhaps the most significant factor in bringing about an improvement in England's fortunes is the implicit recognition – at last – that coaching and selection, especially at the highest level, are different manifestations of the same problem. Roger Uttley tells of the long haul to improve the national side's skills, fitness and match-management, and Chalkie White writes of the need for a universal purpose in playing style. Further refinements are doubtless on the way, though even a cursory reading of this book will show that it definitely does not constitute *A Celebration of England Rugby Selectors*. It is in the nature of English sportsmen to be fiercely self-critical – and of their followers to be just as vehement in their criticisms of their heroes – and modesty, in this age of hype, is happily still in fashion, as witness the reticence of one of our contributors. He utterly refuses to commit to print the story of the try he scored despite the efforts made to stop him by the distinguished subject of his profile article. Our man held the celebrity at bay by dint of a good, meaty hand-off, but is adamant that, 'It is not for puddens to bang on about how they handed off great men.'

But for the moment, a little chest-beating in general will do no great harm, especially as we can depend upon it that someone, just around the corner, is ready to shoot down any English pretensions. I have never heard it done more neatly than at Lansdowne Road after a match in which Ireland's forwards adapted the better to wind and rain. The result was a clear-cut Irish victory over England, upon whose behalf the theory was advanced at the post-match conference that they had determined to play an open, running game and been betrayed by the lack of a firm pitch.

'And God forbid,' intoned an Irish voice from the back, 'it should ever rain in Dublin.'

TED BARRETT

FOREWORD
The Seeds of Change

BOB HILLER

The last 20 years or so have seen such enormous changes in the game of Rugby Union football that an old player from the 1960s, returning from exile in some distant rugbyless land, would find the whole scene almost unrecognisable. The organisation, administration and playing of the game have all taken gargantuan strides forward (or possibly backward, depending on your viewpoint) during that period. These changes in the game have all taken place at an ever-increasing rate until the present moment when, at international level at least, the game teeters on the edge of a whirlpool of controversy which might eventually engulf it or perhaps even destroy it.

Without doubt the single most contentious issue which continually exercises the minds of the game's administrators is the long-running problem of defining – or rather redefining – the rules of amateurism. I do not believe that there has been a radical change in players' attitudes towards obtaining some kind of reward for their efforts, particularly at international level. In my experience, players have always been keen to improve their lot in terms of the conditions and facilities offered to them, especially with regard to lengthy tours abroad. The vexed question of monetary reward did not often arise simply because there was not a vast amount of money available, in complete contrast to the position today. Yet in my early playing days I found it difficult to grasp the logic behind asking players to pay their own expenses to train at Coventry or Leicester when one week later we would be playing in front of a full house at Twickenham with the Rugby Football Union collecting a small fortune in gate receipts.

The situation continually comes to the boil for two reasons. First, as I have already said, the game is now generating vast amounts of money, all made on the backs of players who receive little material reward for their efforts, and secondly, because of the quite ludicrous demands made on these players in terms of the time and commitment required of them.

Having decided to take the plunge and revise the rules, the authorities continually have to face up to the nagging and seemingly intractable problem of where to draw the line. In this respect they have got themselves into an almighty pickle which they will be lucky to resolve satisfactorily, certainly in the short- or medium-term. Whatever the wording of any definition concerning what is or is not permissible, ultimately it all comes down to a question of interpretation and this is where the problem lies.

It seems to me that any money that a player makes by virtue of his being a rugby personality could be construed as being 'rugby-related', which is one of the key terms involved and is not much different from being paid to play the game. It is also a basic premise that players should not take money directly out of the game and hence should not, for instance, be paid for speaking at rugby club dinners, but I suspect that most rugby clubs would be delighted to add a couple of pounds to the cost of a ticket in order to secure the services of a well-known player.

The final poser to be addressed is that of uniformity of application throughout the rugby-playing world. Here the dilemma is even more intriguing because any lines which are drawn by one national authority will almost certainly have been crossed in many other countries already.

I suspect that we are moving slowly towards a sport which is professional or semi-professional at the top level, however much this is disguised, a path which has already been followed by many other disciplines.

Whatever traumas rugby has and will endure from the slow dilution of the amateur ethic, England's improvements on the field of play have been substantial and undeniable.

My own recollection is that the seeds of this renaissance were sown in the late 1960s, beginning with changes made initially at club level. During the Lions tour of South Africa in 1968 it became very apparent to us all that we, in the British Isles, were lagging behind other countries in terms of the sheer dedication, organisation and 'professionalism' required to achieve success at international level. On that tour we had done well against all the provincial sides but we had been fairly comfortably outclassed in three of the four Tests. It was a salutory lesson to us all and made us realise that changes would have to be made if any of the four home countries were ever going to be in a position to mount a serious and consistent challenge to countries like South Africa and New Zealand.

On my return from South Africa I was elected captain of Harlequins and I decided to put into practice a few ideas which, at the time, were fairly progressive but by today's standards would be considered to be very 'old hat'. The first of these was to have a compulsory weekly floodlit training session based on the now familiar dictum of 'no train – no play'. I also decided that we would have an extended warm-up before the game instead of the customary three press-ups and ten seconds deep breathing which up to that point had constituted the pre-match preparation. Before our first club match of the season, which was played at Twickenham, I duly took all the players out into the west car park and led them in a vigorous warm-up which lasted about 20 minutes. As I took the players back into the changing-room for the final team talk, the heavy breathing and beads of perspiration indicated to me that they were all fired up and raring to go from the first whistle. I had been careful to promote an atmosphere of deep concentration and determination but I hadn't reckoned on the natural wit and resilience of the Quins. Grahame Murray, our prop, broke the spell by slumping himself down on a bench before the pre-match talk and inquiring as to whether he might be permitted to have his half-time orange at that point. Colin Payne followed this up by announcing that, at his age, he felt that in future he would only be able to manage the warm-up *or* the second half, but certainly not both. I subsequently discovered that, while all this was going on, one of the other players was being sick in the showers as a result of overexertion, so perhaps I had overdone the pace at which I had introduced these 'revolutionary' techniques.

1968 was also the year when I was selected to play for England and thus I became initiated into the mystique surrounding the preparation for internationals. My first match was against Wales at Twickenham and to prepare for the game we were all billeted at the Lensbury Club in Teddington, meeting there on Thursday night. On the Friday we had a short run for about an hour or so, and on Friday evening we were all taken to *The Black and White Minstrel Show* (in Paris the pre-match entertainment was a visit to the *Folies Bergères* – no wonder we seldom beat France away). On returning to Lensbury most of the team retired to bed, but it had always been my custom to have a leisurely couple of pints at the local on a Friday night before a game and it didn't seem sensible to break the habit of a lifetime even on this occasion. In company with a kindred spirit in the team, I slipped down the road to the local pub, The Tide End Cottage. Having ordered up our drinks we were then devastated to discover that the whole of the England Selection Committee had had exactly the same idea and were seated at the next table. In fact, they didn't seem to mind and rather generously bought us a round of drinks before we all packed off to bed at closing time.

The occasion of one's first cap is always rather special and the excitement of it all dominates the general impression, but at the same time one becomes aware, slowly, of the Rugby Football Union's legendary generosity towards the players. It always seemed quaint to me that players in internationals at that time were supplied with jerseys and socks but not shorts and certainly not boots. Many subsequent discussions between players and officials had failed to change this policy, or the question of post-match accommodation. After the match the players, together with wives or girlfriends (or sometimes both), jumped into the team coach to travel to the Hilton where the evening's festivities were to take place. Invariably we arrived there to find that accommodation had only been booked for the 15 players, plus reserves, which presented a considerable problem. The logistics of fitting 40 people into 20 beds became the most exciting part of the evening and provided the ultimate test of your partner's fidelity.

The evening itself was always enjoyable because, at that time, England changed the team for every match and we were all pretty certain that the cap gained that day would be our last, so we all determined to enjoy ourselves while we had the chance. In the morning we signed the bill and left the hotel.

On one occasion the man at reception explained that there was an excess on my bill and would I mind paying it. I could not understand what it was for because I had not ordered anything against my room number.

'Did you have continental or English breakfast?' he inquired.

'Well, neither actually,' I replied, 'why do you ask?'

'Well, sir,' he said, 'the RFU have directed that if players have an English breakfast they must pay for it themselves.' Things could only get better!

After that first game we gradually became more professional in our approach, a process which culminated with the build-up to our match at Twickenham against South Africa in 1969. The squad trained together at their own expense on several occasions in the weeks leading up to the match. I was appointed captain well in advance of the announcement of the rest of the side and Don White was made official coach – the first man ever to hold that position I believe.

All of this thought and preparation produced the result that we all cherished, the first victory over South Africa by England in 63 years. We all hoped that we had started the ball rolling in the right direction but in truth England were never able to produce any consistency of performance until Bill Beaumont's Grand Slam side of the early '80s.

I think the achievements of the late '60s and the '70s are best summed up in a recent conversation I had with 'Piggy' Powell, the Northampton and England prop. We had been talking about the phenomenal success rate of Simon Hodgkinson when kicking at goal for England.

'Of course,' said Piggy, 'the trouble in our day was that we had such a bad side that we only got into the opposition's half two or three times in the game for you to kick at goal.'

Tongue in cheek I replied: 'You're right, Piggy. If they had had a better side I'd probably still be playing now!'

To which he responded: 'If they had had a better side, neither of us would have been in it.'

Bob Hiller

14

ENGLAND'S RUGBY REFORMATION

CHRIS JONES

For England, the mid-1960s established a cycle of underachievement that would, over the next three decades, reap all the dubious rewards of repeated failure. Wallowing in mediocrity at the halfway point of a ten-year period would become the norm, and the situation was constantly highlighted by quite outstanding individual triumphs for an English game that would be based firmly on the County Championship until the Divisional competition was revived in 1985.

With no League structure in the '60s and '70s, the title of England's top club was left to the arguments and counter claims of the debating tables in bars all over the country. England did not adopt a national squad system until the 1969–70 season and reviews of the season's efforts in rugby record books of this period could only refer to the game's health 'in the North/South/West/Midlands' etc., on a purely regional basis.

It was all very 'established'. England would be awful in those middle seasons of a decade and the Calcutta Cup was lost to Scotland for the first time in 14 years in 1964. Just a single draw was achieved that season and England used 26 players, including three scrum-halves and a total of 13 new caps. The magnificent British Lions triumph in New Zealand in 1971 did not lift English fortunes – they lost all their matches, for the first time, in the winter of 1971–72. Yet they set the game alight with wins against South Africa in Johannesburg in 1972 and New Zealand in Auckland in 1973. John Pullin, the hooker, was then able to bask in the glory of having captained his country to victory over all three major southern hemisphere nations when Australia lost at Twickenham later that same year.

The game as a whole in England was at that time progressing at a measured pace with a trickle of new clubs emerging to enable the Rugby Football Union to show that between 1975 and 1990 the number affiliated to the central body rose from 1,850 to 2,000. Don Rutherford, the RFU's technical administrator, started a playing career that would earn him the England full-back jersey in the

1950s and which has lasted more than two decades with the Union. He has seen the movement for change gradually win over the block vote of the county constituent bodies on whom the game is based in England. The roller-coaster ride taken by the national team each decade convinced a group of strong-minded men that something radical had to be done to steady a ship that, in playing numbers alone, was the biggest in the world. Rutherford explained: 'In the 1960s there wasn't the same kind of travel we now associate with the game and an Easter tour to the West Country was the big event. Now it is tours around the world that interest clubs and players.

'The County competition was very prominent in the '60s and '70s and player loyalty was much stronger. An ambitious player would move to a club with a stronger fixture list and the absence of a League structure meant those fixtures would be kept no matter how good or bad the season.

'It was decided to introduce a Divisional Championship in 1977 but this was quickly shot down by the counties and that was the reaction to any radical change which threatened the County Championship's standing in the English game. Getting agreement for change was a bit like pulling teeth.'

While the counties stood firm amid calls for change designed to improve the national team, there was a radical movement starting, which the game could not affect.

'The early '70s had seen the effects of comprehensive schooling, with the grammar schools disappearing and sixth-form colleges taking the place of as many as five different schools,' said Ron Tennick, the RFU's Assistant Technical Administrator (RFU Schools Union). 'You were seeing five schools being lost along with their teams and only one emerging. That sixth-form college had to look around for someone to play against. Then, of course, came the teachers' strike and it had a tremendous effect on all sport in schools in the 1980s.'

When Tennick started his involvement in 1972 there were 700 schools affiliated to the RFU and now that figure has climbed to 2,700. That appears to counter Tennick's own argument that schools rugby has been severely hit, but statistics can be very misleading.

'We have tried to find out just how many schools are actually playing the game or even just coaching it, but this has proved to be very difficult,' he said. 'Some schools don't want to say they are not playing or coaching because they are afraid of losing their allocation of international tickets! But there is no question that there is an overall decline in the numbers playing rugby at this level.'

The RFU reacted to this extremely worrying decline with large injections of cash allowing the introduction of Youth Development Officers. The first YDO started work in 1989 and two years later he had been joined by another 30 YDOs, all charged with the task of taking up the slack created by the loss of schools rugby. The RFU also turned to its own clubs, asking each to set

DON RUTHERFORD – 'GETTING AGREEMENT FOR CHANGE A BIT LIKE PULLING TEETH'

up sections to help coach and organise. If the game were to continue a steady growth, then crucial ground work had to be done.

Soccer in England had seen the shape of things to come much earlier and Rutherford said: 'The Football Association League clubs run centres of excellence and they have 40,000 other clubs in membership. We have 2,000 growing at a steady rate but it means we start from a long way back. However, the signs are very encouraging and interest in the game is tremendous with up to 1,000 boys and girls attending special one-day courses.'

These youngsters are now offered New Image rugby which allows boys and girls to compete on the same terms, with handling and running the key elements. Flexibility in attitude and application has been shown and, despite the continued opposition of many counties, radical change has been brought about in the senior arena as well.

League rugby started in the 1980s, together with another go at the Divisional Championship. Totally unsuccessful tours to South Africa and New Zealand and the use of 50 England players in a 12-month period during 1984 and 1985 had brought back memories of previous decades of disappointment, but the Championship still stirs mighty argument. The England selectors want to see a series of trials and so the competition survives. This particular argument has been strengthened by the 1991 Grand Slam which even suggested an end to the roller coaster riding. The 1991 triumph had come 11 years after Bill Beaumont's team had ended the depressing mid-'70s in style.

With important moves being made at schools and youth levels and now a structured season for the seniors, it seems certain the steady rise of Rugby Union in England will continue and there could even be a full decade of achievement to help promote the game. It hasn't been an absolute necessity over the last 30 years, but a change would be nice.

JEREMY GUSCOTT – NO 'BY THE BOOK' PLAYER

WELSH VIEW
The Faldo Method

BRIAN PRICE

In 14 years of rugby involvement at Services, college and club levels, I have had the chance to play rugby everywhere from Redruth's 'Hell's Corner' to Gosforth and Northern among the Geordies, and from Liverpool in the west to Thurrock in the east. This, plus my international career, gives me a fair fund of knowledge with which to attempt an objective assessment of the strengths and weaknesses of English rugby.

Neither the plusses nor the minuses in the English game are stable: they shift ground regularly as the sport develops. Recently there has been a vast improvement in England at the highest level, both in performance and administration. In turn, this has caused problems which could destroy all the excellent work achieved, simply because one section wants to move quickly – the players pressing for monetary rewards – whereas the administrators wish to take a more conservative approach to defend the amateur status of the game. The fear is that the players' attention will be focused on commercial success rather than on the actual playing of the game. It is not a problem which is peculiar to England, but because of the traditional stance of the Rugby Union it is likely to have more disastrous results in this country than anywhere else.

The season of 1991 contained the first murmurings of this dilemma, but it was not serious enough to upset the excellent results gained by this present squad of players. So with the strains of 'Swing Low, Sweet Chariot' still ringing in my ears after the final victory of a Grand Slam season, it is a perfect time to attempt an assessment of England's standing, as seen by an envious spectator domiciled west of Offa's Dyke.

Although my association with English rugby stretches back over four decades, it is necessary to study the present set-up to assess accurately whether the powers that be are in fact on the right road. In Wales at the moment we are green with envy over the progress England have made, especially as their 1991 victory robbed us of the record we were so proud of, since Wales had been unbeaten by England at the Arms Park for 28 years. Media criticism is taken far more seriously by today's players than in my time. The fiercest – or most comical, as I saw it – passage written about me was by a very accomplished journalist who described my attempt at a dropped goal as: 'The back end of a pantomime horse trying to play Hamlet.' Criticisms of the present England side range from the kindest – which hold that it is the most efficient machine produced by England, and one which could match the All Blacks – to the cruellest – inevitably originating from the non-England-based media, which claim that the side is devoid of expression and relies totally on a ponderous jumbo pack. My estimation falls somewhere between these extremes, and fits perfectly with my theory about English rugby, which is that the game in England, even at this, the highest level, looks very much the result of learning the sport from a text book. It compares with the way the golfers Severiano Ballesteros and Nick Faldo play their game. Faldo has physically concentrated on learning a new swing that, after years of sweat, brought big dividends, whereas Ballesteros has relied on natural talent which deserts him from time to time. I would like to be Faldo's bank manager, as long as I was free to watch Ballesteros play.

I believe this formal approach to rugby is true of the game in England as a whole and has been enhanced by the increase seen in coaching since the introduction of League rugby. Whether this is viewed as a weakness or not depends on how individuals see the psychology of the game. I tend to think the game should be played in a less rigid strait-jacket, with more individual flair being allowed to express itself, as seen in the best of the French sides, or, if anyone has a memory long enough, how Wales played our game during the '60s and '70s.

To support my argument I would present two pieces of evidence which close study of England's record over my 40 years in and around rugby will support. First, apart from Jeremy Guscott and occasionally Rory Underwood, the present squad play very much by the book. Hill, Carling and Rob Andrew may be ruthlessly efficient but they are also extremely predictable and lack spontaneity in their play. Looking back, this theory is supported by the scant number of innovative players who come easily to mind. Dave Duckham, Bev Risman, Richard Sharp, Peter Jackson and more recently Simon Halliday could have graced any of the sides who traditionally tended to play the game 'off the cuff', and I concede that there are others who could go on the list, but not many.

Secondly, because it takes years to learn the game in this way – rather than it being a natural process – there tend to be frustratingly long gaps between the periods of success. The '50s was the best decade to date for English rugby in more recent times. Two Triple Crown seasons in '54 and '60 sandwiched a Grand Slam in '57, the first since 1928. To achieve that Grand Slam, England used the centre pairing of Butterfield and Cannell (the latter played his first international in 1948), Marques and Currie were in the second season of their long association, and Dickie Jeeps was on his way to a collection of 24 caps. I think this helps to prove my theory that longevity in the wearer of an England jersey is a useful quality if success is to follow. But another 23 years were to go by before England were able to field a XV that was old enough in experience to win a Grand Slam title. Indeed, the '60s and '70s involved two whitewashes, something we in Wales avoided by the thickness of the try-line in 1991; but in the last of these in 1976, four of the England 1980 Grand Slam pack were already learning their lines.

Thus, the compensating advantage of this approach is that the long-term success of the team is almost guaranteed. However, given the large numbers of players involved in the game in England at any one time, you would expect the successful periods to be much closer together. Indeed, there are signs that something is being done to shorten these time spans, and that is of great concern to us Welsh and our Gallic cousins, the French. We both rely on the spasmodic emergence of talent, something which is not even visible on the horizon in Wales as I write.

The great strength of English rugby is what keeps the supply-line running to develop experienced sides: the rich vein of talent coming from the public school system. This has remained constant whereas the Welsh feeding stations of the local grammar schools that were Max Boyce's mythical outside-half factories have all been swallowed up in the all-consuming comprehensive system. Add to this public school system some of the names involved in coaching at that level and you can see a bedrock established for years to come. Roger Uttley, Mike Davis, Welshman Terry Cobner and, until recently, Ian McGeechan of Scotland are all masters influencing the rugby input at these schools.

The decade since Bill Beaumont's Grand Slam may not have been very productive on the playing side, but it incorporated the development of a superb administrative system. It seems to an outsider that English rugby has gone from being a floundering giant to an efficient machine in a comparatively short time.

The evidence for this is the introduction of a complex League structure – which has become the backbone of the game – the development of the coaching organisation from HQ, the help and encouragement for clubs to reorganise themselves, and, although it may now be losing some of its impact, the introduction of the Divisional Championship, which was exactly what was needed to replace the defunct County Championship.

All this positive work was progressing while we in Wales were busy shooting ourselves in the foot at regular intervals. The result is that, provided the player power in England can be mellowed and the conservatism of the 'true blue amateur' at HQ can be broken down somewhat, there is every reason to believe that English rugby is at the beginning of a very exciting period.

MIKE DAVIS – 'ESTABLISHING A BEDROCK'

To be hyper-critical, all that is needed now is to put that coaching manual at the back of the shelf and let the game develop the players for you. Of course, we could allow you to import Max Boyce, but I do think that at the present time our need is greater than yours.

Finally, to extend the debate a little, here is an England team chosen from my 40 years of playing and watching, which I believe would beat Carling's Grand Slam champions:

R. HILLER

P. B. JACKSON   M. S. PHILLIPS   D. J. DUCKHAM   K. J. FIELDING

R. A. W. SHARP   R. E. G. JEEPS

C. R. JACOBS   J. V. PULLIN   M. J. COULMAN

R. W. D. MARQUES   A. M. DAVIS

D. P. ROGERS   W. G. D. MORGAN   P. G. D. ROBBINS

England's record against Wales
P97 W38 L47 D12

PETER JACKSON
England Wing 1956–63

DAVID GREEN

Wingers may come and wingers may go, but Peter Jackson of Coventry, Warwickshire, England and the British Lions will surely always be numbered among the greatest of them, for his play was regularly touched with a unique genius.

The term 'genius' is applied, and with complete justice in my view, to Barry John and Gerald Davies, but they both differed from Jackson in that their supremacy was based on the perfect execution of orthodox manoeuvres. Davies' sidestep, inward and outward feint, and change of pace, and John's lovely hands, his timing of the pass, his uncanny eye for the narrowest gap, were all skills to which other players might at least aspire. However, when Jackson was attacking he defied imitation. The unorthodox, and even the incredible, became almost the norm. Gerald Davies, moving up the right touch-line, would be aiming to score on the right, but there was no guarantee of this with Jackson.

A friend who watched almost the whole of Jackson's career, or more accurately his appearances at Coundon Road, has said to me: 'I wish I had a quid for every time I've seen him suddenly shoot in from the right, cut through half a side and touch down in the left corner. You'd think, well, that's that, he's going to get buried, but there he was, still weaving and wobbling, and sure enough he'd score, and nobody could work out how the devil he'd got there.'

Physically, Jackson was not strong-looking. His pallor, deep-set eyes and dark brows, combined with high cheek-bones and a notably severe hairstyle, gave him an Eastern European aspect, so it was not surprising that he was known to his fellow players as 'Nikolai'. Appearances, though, were deceptive, for he played his rugby at not far short of 12st 7lb, a useful weight 35 years ago when few forwards were much above 15st. His defensive skills were of a high order, for he was extremely difficult to wrong-foot and he tackled low and very firmly. Indeed, his international opponents found him hard to pass. In his 20 games for England, his opposite number scored only twice, C. L. Davies touching down after Clem Thomas had hacked on a loose ball at Twickenham in 1956 and Dewi Bebb getting the only try of the match at the Arms Park in 1959. It is as an attacker, though, that he will be forever remembered and revered. In those days of comparatively low scoring, Jackson's individual tally of six tries mark him as a real danger man, for in his 20 games England scored only 22 tries in all.

He was an awkward player to line up for a tackle, for his upright running action and high knee-lift made for sharp and frequent changes of course in either direction, and he also possessed a most deceptive body swerve. Though not a true flier in the Ken Jones mould, his natural pace was considerable. In Paris in 1958 he robbed a French forward of the ball inside his own 25 and raced fully 80 yards to score, all pursuit being in vain.

His international career began against Wales at Twickenham in 1956, during one of the most successful periods in English rugby. In the four Championship seasons from 1952 to 1955, England had lost only four matches. In 1956, therefore, the selectors might have been excused had they opted for 'the mixture as before', but to their credit they took notice when a young 'possibles' side outplayed the 'probables' in the final trial. Sale and Lancashire hooker Eric Evans, whose international career had seemed to be over, had been put in charge of the 'possibles' and he duly found himself appointed captain of an England side which contained no fewer than ten new caps, of which Jackson was one.

The first result was not auspicious, for Wales won at Twickenham. France also won in Paris but the new-look side secured comfortable victories over Ireland and Scotland. Jackson, who scored his first try for England in the win over Ireland, really made his mark the following season when a dour 3–0 win at Cardiff set England on their way to the Grand Slam. In the next match, against Ireland at Lansdowne Road, he fielded Andy Mulligan's attempted touch-kick and, carrying the ball straight at the Irish pack, threaded his way past several forwards and touched down near the corner. A fortnight later, when France were beaten at Twickenham, he scored two tries, the first when he bamboozled the defence with two sudden changes of direction and the second when he made an orthodox run-in after W. P. C. Davies had broken through.

England almost achieved the Grand Slam again in 1958, but Scotland unexpectedly managed a 3–3 draw at Murrayfield, so they had to content themselves with the Five Nations Championship. Earlier, though, Jackson had figured prominently in a famous victory over the touring Australians at Twickenham. England had been in trouble for most of the match, playing with 14 men for the last 50 minutes, fly-half Phil Horrocks-Taylor having been injured. Moreover, Jim Hetherington played on while badly concussed, and Jeff Butterfield and Peter Thompson were badly knocked about: but

with the score at 6–6, and Butterfield acting as fly-half and open-side Peter Robbins in the centre, England's seven forwards won a line-out. They moved the ball right, but it went to ground before reaching Jackson. He picked it up and, though apparently completely hemmed in, contrived to beat Lenehan, Phelps twice and full-back Curley before squeezing over wide out.

1959 was try-less for Jackson, as indeed it was for the whole England side, and he then rather slipped from favour, John Young or Martin Underwood being preferred. He was recalled for the Scotland match at Twickenham in 1961, ignored throughout 1962 but restored for the 1963 season, in which England again carried off the Championship. That was the year of England's last win at Cardiff for 28 years, a match forever treasured in English memory for the try scored by Malcolm Phillips who interpassed spectacularly with Jackson in a move started deep in England's half by Jim Roberts's long throw-in.

Jackson, who had played so brilliantly on the Lions' tour of Australia just four years earlier, was to play no more international rugby. Incidentally, what a feast for the connoisseur that Lions' tour must have been, with Jackson scoring 19 tries and Tony O'Reilly 20!

Jackson's greatness as a player is beyond dispute, for very few had both the ability to beat man after man in set or broken play and provide an unyielding defence. Recently I was discussing the try he scored against Australia with Bob Frame, who played alongside him for years in the centre for Coventry and Warwickshire. 'It didn't surprise any of us,' he said. 'After all, he seemed to do more difficult things than that three or four times a week for us.'

Though a careful-living man, Jackson has had to undergo heart by-pass surgery. However, he remains fit enough to contribute as fully as he has always done to the Coventry Club, which he serves as General Secretary. He also represents them on the Senior Clubs' Committee.

NEW ZEALAND VIEW
The Conspiracy Theory

DON CAMERON

No pilgrim could want for more. As I took my first step through the gates of Twickenham the public address system burst out with the flourishing finale to the *Triumphal March* from *Aïda*, the rich sounds rolling and echoing around the gaunt old stands. My road to Twickenham had been a long one, frustrating too, for any ambition to become the rugby correspondent for my newspaper, the *New Zealand Herald*, had to wait until that amazing man Terry McLean had moved aside. But there I was, revelling in the sights and sounds of my rugby Mecca. I should also mention that the match, the first of the All Blacks' short tour of England and Scotland in 1979, was still a day or two away. And someone decided that some vigorous Verdi would be just the thing to blow the off-season dust out of the PA.

Since then there have been many memories of England rugby and its marvellous headquarters, which have led to a curious mixture of affection and bewilderment. The accent must be on the first noun, for I have had many a friendly argument with a good friend who from time to time rails about what he terms the upper-middle-class influence on England rugby, and how it spreads its influence deep into the soul of the International Rugby Board.

It is difficult to ask a New Zealander for a balanced, as distinct from distanced, view of England rugby. Or at least one of my wrinkled generation. The impact in the years surrounding the Second World War came more from British, rather than English, rugby, but mention of England and Twickenham did stir memories of Cyril Brownlie being ordered from the field in 1925, and of Obolensky scoring those princely tries in 1936 – although we could never quite imagine how a Russian could play rugby for England.

This colonial suspicion had been nurtured a few years before by the vigorous attack on one of New Zealand's most anointed sacred cows, the 2–3–2 scrum, by 'Bim' Baxter, manager of the British side which toured New Zealand and lit an unquenchable flame in 1930. There are still some

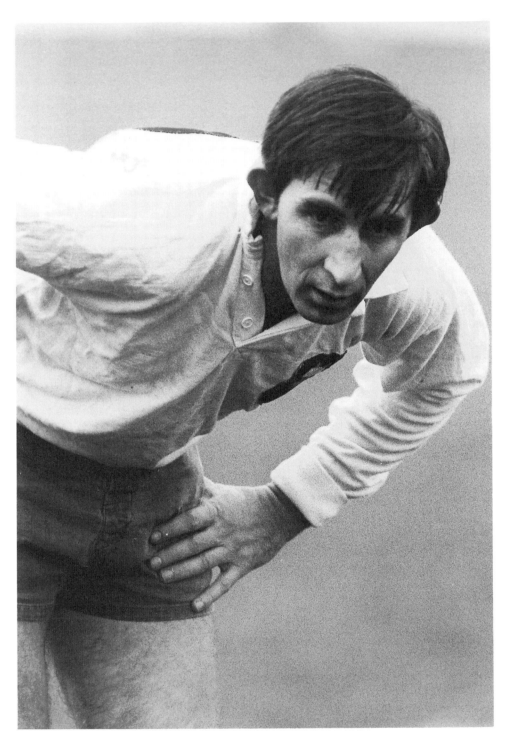

ALAN OLD – KEYSTONE OF NORTHERN TRIUMPH

people around in New Zealand who can explain the virtues of the two-front scrum, and who will maintain that the seven-man scrum led to everything that was great and beautiful in the game, and that New Zealand rugby has never been the same since the infamous Baxter thrust a British knife into its heart. Mind you, there are also those New Zealanders who at the time, and later, maintained that the 2–3–2 scrum could never survive against a powerful 3–4–1 or 3–2–3 pack – as the All Blacks had found in South Africa in 1928 – and that the 'rover' forward thus liberated by the seven-man scrum was in fact an outright cheat and off-side obstructionist. But the feeling was that New Zealand did not fancy a British gentleman criticising what had become such a distinctive part of the New Zealand game.

Ever since, there have been reservations about the New Zealand view of English rugby, even if New Zealanders have for too long tended to identify the RFU and the IRB as very close brothers linking arms against the wishes and ideals of the Colonials across the water. So the English tended to become lumped into the general criticism of the IRB, which every few years would come up with yet another law change which New Zealanders immediately identified as some British plot to remove the latest tactical strength of their country's rugby. Whenever the All Blacks or New Zealand became proficient at some new art, such as rucking the ball from the tackle, kicking penalty goals or devising some line-out skullduggery, it appeared that the IRB, and thus the perfidious English, would immediately bring in some new law to combat the strength. More recently, for example, the modern New Zealand rugby person, quite happy to accept whatever grade of professionalism the market will allow, regards with dismay the RFU's apparent stance against overliberal payments for players. There is still a touch of the them-and-us in the New Zealand attitude to English rugby.

This is an unfortunate gap, but understandable when considering that 12,000 miles represents a wide distance in terms of both geography and sporting philosophy – and are not helped, it might be suggested, by the rather dominating impact of All Black rugby over the last generation drawing persistent sniper fire from what used to be the battlements of Fleet Street. Unfortunate, too, for the divisions tend to diminish when there is first-hand contact from either side. Only then do you find that the aims and ambitions of both sides tend to coincide; that the divisions are mostly matters of imagination.

It is part of my brief that I should mention the England team which has impressed me most. The memory goes back to those gallant pioneers of 1963, an England team very much better, and braver, than a played-five-lost-four record in New Zealand would indicate. Or to that singular England side which outplayed and defeated the All Blacks at Eden Park in 1973, and which had the England reserves raising enormous chants and shouts of encouragement, much to the dismay of the wriggling New Zealand officials a few feet behind them. Or the England side of 1983 which won at Twickenham against an All

SIX LEICESTER PLAYERS IN THE ENGLAND XV v NEW ZEALAND AT TWICKENHAM, NOVEMBER 1983. LEFT TO RIGHT: DUSTY HARE, NICK YOUNGS, PETER WHEELER, LES CUSWORTH, PAUL DODGE AND CLIVE WOODWARD

ENGLAND SCORE THROUGH MAURICE COLCLOUGH'S TRY AT HEADQUARTERS IN 1983: NUMBER 8 IS JOHN SCOTT, 9 NICK YOUNGS, 12 PAUL DODGE, 13 CLIVE WOODWARD AND 1 COLIN WHITE

Black side of modest method – and which had dear old Mickey Steele-Bodger trying his damnedest to be unaffected afterwards.

But the team of Englishmen, as distinct from an England team, which made the greatest impression on me – and which illustrated so much that is good and so much that is infuriating about English rugby – was the Northern Division side which defeated the All Blacks 21–9 at Otley in 1979. Even before the match, played on that grey and wicked day at Cross Green, the occasion had special impact. The one tiresome aspect of a rugby correspondent's life is the need to write previews of matches, with whatever analytical ability suitably balanced by lots of 'ifs' and 'howevers'. Not the *Yorkshire Post* of 17 November 1979. At breakfast the All Blacks were able to read from Bill Bridge: 'Today's thundering clash of the unbeaten All Blacks . . . will be the match when the 20-match winning run for the tourists will come to an end.' Later he did allow that John Carleton, the England wing, might be allowed to play Northern's token amount of running in the last 30 seconds 'by which time victory should be won'.

Mr Bridge was emphatically right, one of the great pieces of sporting journalism. He was right because the Northern Division selectors and their senior players had worked out where the 1979 All Blacks were strong and where they were vulnerable. They decided that the All Blacks could be attacked in midfield through a mixture of smart half-back play, backed by strong support from the loose forwards. They had the wit to read Northern's strengths and the All Black weaknesses, and had the men to make the plan work – Alan Old and Steve Smith in the inside backs, and Tony Neary, Roger Uttley and Peter Dixon in the loose forwards. And work the plan did, a totally admirable mixture of a style of play perfected over the years by various All Black teams, and reassembled brilliantly by the Northern experts. That evening there were no sad All Black tales. Bill Beaumont's men had been decisive and skilled winners, and now his main worry was the Test against England a week hence.

Yet about the same time Beaumont was confessing that the team he would lead on to Twickenham seven days later would be very different in personnel and playing style to the heroes he had led that afternoon. He was right, so depressingly right. The England selectors had to all intents and purposes picked their team and tactics before Cross Green. They made some changes after that famous victory, but still neglected the winning recipe. Of the famous five – Smith, Old, Neary, Dixon and Uttley – who had smashed the All Blacks at Otley, the England selectors picked only Smith and Neary. They discarded Old, Dixon and Uttley, and with them the playing pattern that Beaumont wanted, and which had triumphed. At Twickenham an All Black side, in such turmoil that they played four wing three-quarters in their back line, scrimped and saved until they had a 10–9 win, with Graham Mourie and David Loveridge playing a mini-version of the tactics with which Northern had won.

31

More recently there was a Midlands side which claimed an equally outstanding win over the 1983 All Blacks, and yet could not make suitable impact on England selection or tactics.

There has been, then, a north–south split in England rugby, perhaps even more divisive than the various regional biases in New Zealand rugby. Here centres only a few miles apart could have wildly divergent views on how the game should be played, but this division has been broken down since the National Championship began in 1976, and the various power-centres in New Zealand rugby have much more regular playing contact. Now the regional differences are slight and, given the All Black playing pattern built around John Hart's brilliant direction of the Auckland side in the mid-1980s, the top players are now very familiar with and happy about the consistent attacking style adopted by the national side. Any leading New Zealand player can now move into the All Blacks, content that he knows their basic style and will fit in quite quickly.

In England, by contrast, the styles and philosophies still vary. The change away from the traditional club fixtures toward League competitions and district and regional representative sides will bring to England rugby what the National Championships have done for New Zealand. A reasonably simple and basic playing style will emerge, common to the big clubs of London, to the power-houses in the south-west, and to the wise men of the north.

The strong performance in the 1991 World Cup may be regarded in the future as the great achievement of the decade for England rugby. Better still, perhaps, would be the evolution of the game when their vast playing resources and manpower are being harnessed along one straight and simple and effective playing channel.

It may take five or ten years, but when it comes the rose of England rugby will be in full bloom.

England's record against New Zealand up to the end of the 1991 World Cup
P16 W3 L13

JOHN PULLIN
England Hooker 1966–76

JOHN MASON

For all his caps, successful overseas tours and an uncomplicated, matter-of-fact approach to the captaincy of England, 12 words ensured that John Vivian Pullin possesses an unsurpassed claim to lasting fame.

The occasion was the post-match dinner in Dublin on 20 January 1973, after Ireland, inspired by their forwards and sustained by the accurate kicking of Barry McGann, had briskly dismissed the England challenge in an emphatic 18–9 victory. As Pullin, a rugged farmer well used to the cycles of life and blessed with a dry, sardonic humour, got to his feet to propose the toast to the home team, he waited for the crowded, cheerful room to become silent. Then, the formalities of introduction complete, his measured West Country burr accentuating his words, he said simply: 'We may not be very good – but at least we turn up.' For a fraction longer the room remained quiet. A moment later, as the import of what England's captain had said dawned, every Irishman present was on his feet roaring approval and laughter – and there was the odd tear too. Pullin need not have uttered another word that evening and the freedom of Dublin would still have been his.

At a stroke the astute Pullin, never known to use two words where one would do, had reassured his hosts that, threat of terrorist action or not, England would continue to play international matches in Ireland. Whatever reasons, no matter how well-based, Wales and Scotland may have had the previous season for declining to play in Dublin, England did not share that view.

Years later the modest Pullin, who farms at Aust in the shadow of the Severn Bridge on the Gloucestershire bank of the river, insisted that the deeper implications of his remark were a happy accident. All that he had intended to do was to raise a smile among his many Irish friends as well as gently chiding his colleagues for a less than forthright display. When it is appreciated that the England side that afternoon included David Duckham,

33

Stack Stevens, Fran Cotton, Roger Uttley, Peter Dixon, Andy Ripley and Tony Neary, Pullin could be excused for keeping his more critical opinions for the relative privacy of the dressing-room and training pitch.

Barely six months previously the adept Pullin, who came to the Bristol club in the 1960s at about the time John Thorne, another international hooker, was thinking of stepping aside, had led England to victory over South Africa at Ellis Park in Johannesburg – coincidentally also by 18–9. By the following September, this time at Eden Park in Auckland, the city of sails, England had beaten the All Blacks too, with Pullin in charge. If pressed thereafter, he conceded that perhaps England were not that bad, after all. As he represented his country 42 times, in addition to seven appearances for the Lions against South Africa (three) and New Zealand (four), in 1968 and 1971 respectively, the opinions of the much-travelled Pullin could be said to carry some weight.

And mention of weight is a reminder that Pullin, whose early rugby days were at Thornbury Grammar School and Bristol Saracens, the Bristol and District Combination club, never had any problems about the demands made on his sturdy frame in the twilight world of the front row. An outdoor life in all weathers – it can blow an icy gale off the Severn seemingly at any time of the year – gave him a natural fitness. Nor did anyone willingly arm or wrist wrestle with Pullin, such was the strength of his muscular arms and large capable hands.

There was an easy agility, too, a speed off the mark and ball skills that surprised many an opponent. Remember it was Pullin who sustained the early passage of the ball in *that* try scored by Gareth Edwards for the Barbarians against the All Blacks. For those of us who had the good fortune to watch Pullin (who was 50 in January 1991) grow up rugby-wise, such athletic authority was no surprise. The Bristol club, though ideally suited, did not play much seven-a-side rugby in those days. Had they done so, Pullin would have been every bit as effective as latter-day runners and handlers such as Peter Wheeler or John Olver, sevens experts and international hookers who had flirted with the back row in their playing youth.

Fortuitously, before abandoning a general reporter's desk in Bristol in the late 1950s for a Press Association job in London, I rolled inexpertly around the local pitches of the lower teams. On one such afternoon a shrewd local referee, the late Stan Johnson, told me enthusiastically about two Combination youngsters bursting with talent. One was ambitious, the other kept his own counsel. Perhaps a little publicity in the *Evening Post* Green 'Un, the Saturday evening sports edition – begging the *Telegraph*'s pardon, still my favourite newspaper – would stir a few feet, preferably in the direction of the Bristol club itself? By the time I returned to Bristol five years later in my new role as *Evening Post* rugby correspondent, I swiftly discovered that Stan Johnson, as ever, had got it right again. Both were progressing famously. The shy one? J. V. Pullin of Bristol Saracens,

previously a student at the Royal Agricultural College, Cirencester. His Saracens colleague? Mike Collins, one of the more vigorous wings I have encountered, who played for Bristol, Gloucestershire and, later on, Rosslyn Park. Opponents tended to know when Collins was around.

For a long time in those early Bristol days it was claimed that Mike did all John's talking. Certainly on the longer away journeys – Bristol usually travelled by road and the reporter was part of the group – they tended to be together, with England's captain-to-be fast asleep for hours at a time. Pullin, a powerful scrummager with those long, strong legs flicking effortlessly for the ball, did his talking, as it were, on the field. He was also in the first batch of first-class hookers who appreciated the value of the line-out throw, a skill that while not escaping him, was never the pride of an otherwise immense repertoire. Previously wingers had thrown in.

Yet whatever the technocrats might say, Pullin's appearance record for England and the Lions speaks for itself . . . and this was the man whom England had dropped after his first cap against Wales at Twickenham in 1966. England, I know, were delighted that he, too, turned up after that initial slap in the face. Somehow, he was not quite so shy either.

SIMON HODGKINSON – ENGLAND'S GRATITUDE

SCOTTISH VIEW
No Cameras at Flodden

NORMAN MAIR

On a wet March afternoon at Murrayfield in 1950, Tommy Gray, Scotland's full-back who had lost half a foot in Hitler's war, converted a try by Donald Sloan to give Scotland a spine-tingling 13–11 victory. Scotland were not to beat England again until Jim Telfer's Match in 1964 when that now famed forwards' coach, operating from number 8, gave the last pass for two of Scotland's three tries and scored the other.

Those barren years explain a large proportion of Scotland's deficit versus the original enemy, the Sassenachs having won 52 matches to the 39 of Scotland, with 17 drawn. Nevertheless, in those 13 seasons when England never knew defeat at the hands of the Scots, there were some desperately close-run encounters including the draw earned by Andy Hancock's never-to-be-forgotten last-minute try, a moment doubly assured of immortality by the bellowing of a purpling old blimp in the stand as the exhausted Hancock collapsed over the Scottish line in the corner to beat Iain Laughland's despairing tackle: 'Round behind the posts, you bloody fool!'

In 1963 at Twickenham, a ground which ranks in Scottish affections somewhere below the poll tax, Scotland jumped quickly into a heady 8–0 lead . . . a try from that dark and satanic scourge of stand-offs, the Dunfermline open-side flanker, Ronnie Glasgow, which was converted by Stan Coughtrie, and a dropped goal by the legendary Ken Scotland who was at stand-off that day . . .

'Those eight points will make it a much better game,' nodded the Englishman sitting next to me with satisfaction. That Englishman was the much respected rugby correspondent of the *Sunday Telegraph*, Michael Melford, and, blast him, he was absolutely right. The blond thoroughbred that was Richard Sharp thrillingly won the match for England with one of the great tries of rugby lore – a try the BBC showed so often on television as to leave every Scot merely thankful that they had not had their cameras at Flodden.

One cites that comment by Melford because it catches perfectly the difference between the two countries, since there are no circumstances in which an early English lead of eight points could possibly be construed by any Scot as being about to add to the sum of human happiness. It is, one would submit, a difference emanating partly from England's huge advantage in numbers.

It was the late Sir Henry Cotton who captured what was wrong with so much of English sport when the competition grew a lot more fierce with the spread to the outside world of so many games which had formerly been largely the preserve of the home countries: when, in other words, it was no longer just a question of seeking to beat the much smaller nations of Scotland, Ireland and Wales.

'Many,' stated Cotton unequivocally, 'are afraid to be caught trying. I am not.' You could not level that charge at Nick Faldo or so many of his contemporaries, and, similarly, you could not level it at the England of Geoff Cooke, Roger Uttley and Will Carling. Yes, there were always players with a touch of Cotton's ambition about them and, when it was catching, England were apt to be very dangerous. It goes deeper now, though, and no one in the English camp is worried lest they be criticised for taking the game or themselves seriously.

That change of attitude is likely in itself to do much to enable England to take more appropriate advantage of that imposing numerical strength which does so much to ensure that seldom, if ever, will they run as short of the requisite measures of size and pace as the other home countries are always liable to do. But the coming of a National League structure, a concept pioneered in Scotland by what was for long a mere handful of much vilified but intrepid innovators, also represents a sea change. Indeed, though the cup has been for English rugby what the authors of *1066 and all that* would have called 'a very good thing', and not just as a useful money-spinner either, it is their adoption of a fully-fledged National League which their foes fear will make them much more formidable.

Above all, it will give the players, habitually, the competitive edge so many of them have singularly lacked in the past. Again, leagues tend to channel the better players into relatively few clubs, something which always happened in England to a far greater extent than in Scotland but which was still not to be compared with Wales, where, invaluably, so much of the available talent congregated within a small, geographically tight, knot of major clubs.

In the years after the Second World War, England's rugby thinking was light years ahead of Scotland's – partly, but not by any means wholly, because the influence of the universities of Oxford and Cambridge, with their then unrivalled opportunities to plan and practise, was much more immediate. Varsity rugby was then in something of a purple patch. The Oxbridge XVs of those days were peopled with unusually mature students in the persons of ex-servicemen, and they were, too, exposed to the views of a man like

IAN McGEECHAN – ANDREW'S TUTOR ON TOUR

B. H. Travers. That Australian Dark Blue, whom England capped, found much of the tactical and technical outlook in these islands archaic, obsessed – as it was still apt to be – with what England and Scotland, in their respective styles, had done in the vintage stretch each had enjoyed at different periods of the '20s.

The game in Scotland had originally revolved around the schools, and the Former Pupil and Academical clubs served the country nobly in earlier times. Gradually, however, it had become obvious to those who had eyes to see that the game north of the Border was being strangled by the old school tie. In particular, the predominance of closed clubs meant that all too often the talent would be fatally diluted. Those who had yearned for Scotland's national XV to recover at least some of the old glory looked with envy at the great clubs of England and Wales – the Coventrys and the Northamptons, the Cardiffs and the Swanseas.

In truth, it is one of the ironies to many Scots that England, in the shape of the Rugby Football Union, should in recent seasons have been the most resolute of all in taking a stand against the supposed drift towards out-and-out professionalism. Certainly, they can claim to be taking the larger view for, were the game to go professional, England is better placed than most, with quite a few rich clubs capable of drawing a volume of spectator support well beyond any club in Scotland.

Not just today but generally, down the years, England have had big ball-winning packs but, with the evolution of specialisation, there was, it would be impossible to deny, an overemphasis on the set-pieces. Too many of the forwards have not been the all-round rugby players which their All Black counterparts were. Some denizens of the England tight five were wont to do little more than trot from one set piece to the next and there were gifted back-row forwards who were yet too often too loose. Nor was their rucking, and therefore much of their second phase play, in the same class as that of the New Zealanders.

The All Blacks, in the absence of the Springboks, are most often the yardstick by which all countries are measured, but it should be noted that a feature of post-war rugby has been the failure of the British game to match the legerdemain, both fore and aft, of the Tricolors at their best. Particularly up front, much of the secret lay with the donor and the way the ball was at times almost left hanging in the air for the recipient to collect at his leisure, at least by comparison with inter-passing among British packs who had to be taught not to fire the ball at each other like so many rogue missiles. It is not true today but, for long enough after the 1939–45 war, British back play was far ahead of New Zealand's, even if, to modern eyes, some of the passing, founded on the classic swing of the arms and hips, would look a little old-fashioned. England, in the years dating back to the major law changes of the '60s, have never had a back division which produced rugby to match that of Wales in the days of Barry John or Phil Bennett, unless it was the back division of 1990. Yet, they have on sundry occasions had great ability at their disposal if perhaps never a full-back who, whatever his other attributes, could hit the attack as devastatingly as did, in their contrasting styles, J. P. R. Williams or Andy Irvine.

When Murrayfield was opened in 1925, Scotland won the first of their three Grand Slams, but the first points recorded at the ground came from a penalty goal by England's Luddington, the first penalty goal in the Calcutta Cup for 30 years. Nowadays, if they go 30 minutes without a penalty goal it is regarded as a minor miracle – which is why England have had cause to be grateful to Simon Hodgkinson and many before him, stretching back, in one's own case, to Jack Heaton of boyhood memory.

Individually, England have had their share of players whose play trans-cended national frontiers, enriching the rugby afternoons of many of us besides those of their own compatriots. Men like their will o' the wisp wing, Peter Jackson, who could go either way, the trail of fallen bodies in his wake reminiscent of the stakes he used to jink in and out of in his schooldays at Trent College. Or Jeff Butterfield in the centre, whom Fred Allen, the celebrated All Blacks coach, named as the finest passer of a ball he had ever seen. Or Dickie Jeeps, an indestructible competitor at scrum-half. Or David Marques and John Currie, whose combination spoke so eloquently of the value of coupling at lock your principal specialist jumper with a broad-shouldered, hard-working henchman. Or Peter Robbins, who was a superb open-side wing forward and one who, in an injury emergency, could do his stuff as a three-quarter in the defeat of the 1958 Wallabies. Or David Duckham, a mercurial three-quarter of flashing foot-work. Or, at prop, the massive Fran Cotton, who could pack on either head and who was a good enough footballer to figure in England's winning side in the Scottish Rugby Union Centenary Sevens. Or Peter Wheeler, an accomplished hooker and mobile forward, a player of much personality and a worthy successor to the redoubtable John Pullin. Or Bill Beaumont, a lock forward who was yet considered by the Scots to be England's best forward when it came to winning the ball on the ground. And many another besides. Yet, when one turns to the best England XV one has seen, one arrives at the '90s – not at Will Carling's Grand Slam side but rather at the team he led the previous season.

Much has been said and written about how much they learned from their defeat at Murrayfield and the steel it gave them . . . and it is true that like golfers, teams sometimes have to be there more than once before they can translate opportunity into final triumph. However, the Grand Slam side did have Dean Richards back and, though not a traditional number 8, he is a match-winner – in which context, one recalls the 1989 Wallabies letting slip that while they reckoned they could cope with the driving play of either Mike Teague or Richards, they were a lot more doubtful about their capacity to deal with them in tandem.

The main reason England won the Grand Slam in 1991 and not in 1990, though, was that the Scotland match was at Twickenham and not at Murrayfield. In almost every other respect, save ground advantage and the aforesaid – admittedly important – return of Richards, the England of 1990 had it over the England of 1991. Nor does one make that contention merely because they scored 12 tries to three where the Grand Slammers managed a try-tally of but 5–4, with France actually scoring three to England's one on Sassenach soil. Scotland's defeat of England at SRU headquarters in 1990 is rated the greatest win in their bethistled history simply because England were so good in that campaign. Well though Scotland played, they would still have lost but for that superlative tackle by Scott Hastings as Rory Underwood erupted through the middle.

It is a valid reservation concerning both England teams, though, that neither Rob Andrew nor Simon Hodgkinson, for all their invaluable assets in other dimensions of the game, poses all that great a threat in his own right. Otherwise these were both enviably well-equipped, experienced England XVs with size, strength and skill up front, and lashings of pace and ability behind. By 1990, Rob Andrew was twice the player he had been before the 1989 Lions tour, where Ian McGeechan was such an influence on him. More pertinent still, in contributing hugely to that victorious mission Down Under, the England forwards, rightly castigated previously for possession which was abundant 'but slow, static and upright', had digested both the need for much lower body positions on the drive and the desirability of giving maul ball as much as possible of the dynamism of a ball which had been rucked.

The England of '91 seemed at times scared of their own shadows, the legacy, one never doubted, of Murrayfield. Had they beaten the Scots that day, what a side we might have seen doing what only they have done before, namely winning successive Grand Slams.

England's record against Scotland up to the end of the 1991 World Cup
P108 W52 L39 D17

MIKE COLEY – 'A BIT LIKE READING YOUR OWN OBITUARY'

MARKETING MEN AT HEADQUARTERS

CHRIS REA

The first sponsorship deal struck at Twickenham, although the Rugby Football Union was blissfully unaware of it at the time, was in the early '70s when a clock manufacturer offered to install two clocks, one in the middle of the North Stand, the other at the south-east corner of the ground, for a nominal charge, if permission were granted for the company name to be displayed on the clocks. In its naïvety, and thinking that it was getting something for nothing, the RFU readily agreed to the request – so the clock company it was which was getting something for nothing every time the television cameras cut away for a time check.

By the next decade the word sponsorship had become an accepted part of rugby's vocabulary, and the RFU had moved sufficiently far enough forward with the times to recognise the need for professional help with their fund-raising efforts. They hired a marketing and sports sponsorship company, West Nally, a company with an impressive track record in cricket and soccer, and came up with an élite package for sponsors involving hospitality at Twickenham, perimeter-board advertising and space in match programmes. The cost of this package was set at £250,000. Eight élite sponsors were sought but only three took up the offer.

By the mid-'80s, the RFU was receiving £300,000 per annum from their various sponsorship schemes, including a three-year deal with John Player worth £100,000 for the club knock-out cup competition. The other major sponsor at the time, although at a figure significantly lower than John Player, was Thorn EMI, the sponsors of the County and Divisional Championships. But in 1985 the RFU decided that it could generate more income if the sponsorship and marketing jobs were done from within its own organisation rather than through an outside agency, and the post of marketing manager was therefore advertised.

One of the applicants was Mike Coley, whose background in sales and marketing and whose rugby knowledge as a player, referee and active club member of Harlequins, made him an ideal candidate for the job. But Coley did not exactly distinguish himself during the interview at which the RFU's representatives were Albert Agar, the President, Bob Weighill, the Secretary, and the Honorary Treasurer, Sandy Sanders. An interview which had been timed to last half an hour finally ended after an hour and a half, and Coley returned home certain that whoever got the job it would not be him. There had been some heated exchanges between Coley and Sanders as to how the RFU should maximise the increasing popularity of the sport. Coley was adamant that the successful applicant should, within reason, be allowed a certain amount of independence and authority, and he also raised a howl of disbelief by guaranteeing that he would raise £1 million by the second year.

The interview was on a Thursday and on the Saturday morning Bob Weighill telephoned to tell Coley that he had got the job. Unfortunately, no one thought to tell *The Times*, who duly readvertised the post on Monday morning – 'It was a bit like reading your own obituary,' Coley recalls. He accepted the job, though, and agrees that it was one of the best decisions he has ever made. He also acknowledges the massive support and encouragement he subsequently received from his tormentor at the interview, Sandy Sanders.

One of Coley's first acts in his new post was to reprice the élite sponsorship package. Better, he argued, to have eight sponsors at half price than three at the full rate. He then set about making a promotional film and went out to sell the RFU to potential sponsors.

The first presentation he made was to Save & Prosper. Everything that could go wrong did. The film broke down, slides were put into the projector upside down and for once Coley was left speechless. The presentation was a disaster, but Coley's enthusiasm and belief in his product succeeded in persuading the company that they should become associated with the game, and they took up one of Coley's repriced élite packages. By the next Five Nations [see Sponsorship chapter] Save & Prosper increased that involvement substantially when they agreed to be the RFU's major sponsor for international matches at Twickenham.

There were other major developments taking place within the game. John Player were replaced by Pilkington as sponsors of the Cup, and Toshiba took over the County and Divisional Championships from Thorn EMI. But the most exciting venture was the establishment of the National League structure involving more than 1,100 clubs in England. It was new territory and no one was quite certain of its worth. There was no doubt of the potential of such a structure, and the success of the Leagues in Scotland, where they were by now well established, offered considerable encouragement to the RFU, but it was a gamble nevertheless.

Courage, the brewing company, had expressed an interest in sponsoring the Leagues, and Coley remembers going into the meeting with no fixed idea of a figure to place on the sponsorship. But his argument that the RFU should go in high and negotiate down prevailed. The figure for the first year was therefore pitched at £½ million. The RFU held its breath, Courage went out to deliberate and the result was a three-year deal, including an élite package at Twickenham, totalling £1.7 million. It has been a superb sponsorship and Courage, delighted with the success of the Leagues and with the public response, entered their second three-year agreement worth £2.5 million.

The money is pouring into the RFU's coffers: £850,000 per annum from the élite sponsors; £150,000 from perimeter advertising; and from the hospitality boxes which, by some shrewd manoeuvring in the four corners of the ground, Coley has managed to increase to 104, £1.6 million.

Merchandising is another rapidly increasing source of income with potential for even greater growth. In Coley's first year the RFU shop which shares accommodation with the museum had an annual turnover of £35,000. Now resited behind the West Stand, it is one of the busiest areas at Twickenham on match days. In the month following England's Grand Slam victory, goods worth £100,000 had been sold, and the annual turnover is now somewhere in the region of £½ million.

Is there no end then to the success story? Coley thinks there is. He believes that saturation point has almost been reached in most of the conventional areas of fund-raising. There are, however, many other lucrative avenues still to be explored. Twickenham remains one of the RFU's most valuable assets, yet it is grossly underused. With the advent of the European series in American football played mainly throughout the summer months when Twickenham is lying fallow, Coley could generate a substantial income, and, if plans go ahead to widen the pitch, it would also be possible to accommodate international soccer. Whether or not the RFU would ever permit professional sport to be played on the ground is another matter, but, as their marketing manager, Coley sees it as his duty to inform the RFU of the opportunities open to them, this option remains to be considered.

With an annual income to the RFU of £4 million, though, Coley's targets have been reached. Coley, who left the RFU late in 1991, had delivered much more than he promised during that fateful interview in 1985, in what has probably turned out to be the most profitable 90 minutes the Rugby Football Union ever spent.

CASH AND THE CLUBS
The Moseley Million

MICHAEL BLAIR

Since the Second World War, Rugby Union has been through a number of revolutions, the most obvious being in its attitudes to the playing of the game and the licence it gives to its players. Fitness standards are higher, technical awareness is keener and the very philosophy on which the game is founded is under attack. But in no sphere of rugby football is there more profound upheaval than in its financial structuring. It took a long time and it is still blinkered and confused, but rugby has finally entered the commercial world.

Vast profits are generated by international rugby at the big venues (£600,000 a time at Twickenham, for instance) and much of the money is ploughed back into the grass roots by the various Rugby Unions. But the clubs, the backbone of the game, have to make their own way and here we enter the realms of shoestring economics. Rugby, in some of its areas, lives by what is put into the beggar's bowl. It lives by sponsorship, and we can take Moseley FC, one of England's oldest clubs, as a prime example of how the wheels of commerce turn.

In 1949, which is a random year, Moseley's season cost them £1,667, including £387 for match expenses and travelling. The money came from four simple sources. The bulk, all of £833, was raised by subscriptions and members' donations. They took £659 at the gate and £175 from programme sales, canteen and bar, which suggests that the club members were a somewhat abstemious collection at the time. In their accounts as presented in April 1991, Moseley's annual expenditure had soared to £228,629 and their income to £216,000, a loss – and this was not usual – of more than £12,000, thanks partly to the fact that match and travelling expenses were heavy – £80,000. This was the result of all Pilkington Cup matches being drawn away, and none at home. If the fixed assets of the club are taken into account, the club finances encompass a total of more than £1 million annually. Staff wages amount to

£43,000, since there is a full-time club-manager and a groundsman, plus a professional playing and coaching administrator.

As Moseley entered the 1950s, they were showing figures that will amuse us now: match expenses and travelling, £387; groundsman's wages, upkeep of ground and repairs, £489; and – this will make today's treasurers hoot – footballs, jerseys and equipment, £15. You won't get many pairs of bootlaces for £15 today.

Thanks to their run of away cup matches, Moseley's gate and programme sales receipts after the 1991 season showed a significant drop from £33,399 to £23,586, but membership subscriptions were higher at £26,419. In the previous season the bar surplus of £17,000 cast a profound gloom over the club because the figure was some £15,000 short of what it should have been. That money could not be accounted for and police internal investigations were carried out, the whole sorry affair pointing to the necessity for clubs to develop an administrative structure appropriate to the amount of money involved. As it is Moseley pay out £29,642 for administration and general expenses and they have no fewer than 26 honorary officials within the club. In 1949, Moseley's nett bill for rent, rates and taxes amounted to £144. Today, their rates come to nearly £8,826. Heat, light and water, which cost a mere £55 in 1949, puts £14,923 on the expenditure and an annual maintenance and repair bill can come to nearly £30,000. Whereas once the après match repast was a plate of beans or a dollop of bangers and mash, players are much more sensitive about their diets. Included in Moseley's playing expenses is a sum of £11,000 for feeding the team. And, as exotic tours are now, apparently, obligatory, the club gave £7,000 towards the cost of the 1990 tour of Texas. Players have to be kept happy, which is one of the more cynical developments of rugby football. It is doubtful if any balance sheet in the land will show, precisely, what is paid to get players to training and to matches, and Moseley are not an exception.

They are undoubtedly one of rugby's 'cleaner' clubs, in that they do not offer the sort of financial inducements that are attributed to some clubs in England and plenty in Wales. But they did report in their last accounts that match allowances had risen by £2,000. It is always a tough and sometimes a delicate task to steer a rugby club through today's financial minefields.

Moseley's financial structure was transformed in 1979 by the appointment to their committee of a Worcestershire hotelier, Greville Edwards. Beyond a natural enthusiasm for the game, Edwards knew little about rugby and less about conventional committee work. But he did have a rare knack of making money, which Moseley slowly came to realise. So they appointed Edwards their honorary fund-raising officer, gave him a small committee and sat back to count the profits.

Club rugby was into commerce and the effects have been profound. Edwards had a high regard for his own ability as a salesman; and he has a philosophy. If he can sell something to himself, then he can sell it to anybody. He promptly sold himself a ground perimeter hoarding on which was emblazoned the name of the Barnt Green Inn, a large inn ten miles outside Birmingham which he then owned. He was not merely advertising his inn, he was advertising advertising. The pitch at The Reddings was soon completely encircled. He sold himself a half-page slot in the match programme and again the business houses of Brum followed suit. In the first season following Edwards' appointment, Moseley were the richer by £2,500 from their extraneous earnings. There was no stopping Edwards now.

A friend of his in Worcester owned a portacabin which he was prepared to let. Edwards transported it to The Reddings, let it as a hospitality suite which could house between eight and ten people and charged £75 a time, paying his friend £16 of that. Soon there was another box and Edwards bought a job-lot of chairs from a Sunday school at £1.50 each with which to furnish it. Today, there are nine hospitality boxes, plushly furnished, and the club will put up a marquee at the drop of an enquiry. Their average charge per head in 1990–91 was £30 – for an afternoon (and sometimes an evening!) that includes food, drink, car parking and a First Division match. 'If you get your package right, people automatically want to come back again,' said Edwards. It is Moseley's boast that they can accommodate any number between eight and 180, and they have never refused a client. In all, there are nine sponsorship packages on offer at The Reddings and Moseley even started to let their committee room for a new enterprise, match sponsorship.

Match sponsorship started at £350 a time and there were five sponsors in the first year. There were nine in the second, 18 in the third and now match sponsorship has reached saturation point. Every home Saturday – and sometimes on Wednesdays as well – there are two principal match sponsors at £950 a time, and lesser sponsors too. From Sale, Edwards copied the idea of match ball sponsorship and there are now 70 of these per season at £50 a time.

Sponsorship, of course, is the lifeline that Rugby Union, generally, has grasped. Few saw its significance more clearly than Moseley. Of the £350,000 (the figure is nett, after Edwards' commission) that Edwards raised in the five years of his professional attachment to the club, approaching a half of that has come from major sponsors. In 1990–91 Moseley were indebted to their major sponsor, PE International, for a sum of £27,500, and two associate sponsors added £17,000 between them. Of their income of £212,000 in 1990, approximately half came from sponsorship.

While the Moseleys of the rugby world can attract substantial sponsorship and a relatively healthy return on the gate, we see the same basic money-making methods in junior rugby but obviously on a smaller scale. Veseyans, of the North Midlands League, Division One, who were originally an old boys club connected to Bishop Vesey's School in Sutton Coldfield, are a fairly typical junior set-up who run four sides every Saturday. Even they could show the item 'gate receipts' on their last balance sheet for they reached the semi-finals of the North Midlands Cup and that was worth £200 from the paying customers.

The season cost Veseyans £5,400, and they lost money. Jerseys and balls cost them more than £1,000, after-match meals set them back £650, insurance £422 and they took a loss of more than £700 on their annual dinner. Their income came to £4,500 and for £2,000 of that they were indebted to their sponsors. In all there are seven sponsors and the main one of these, which contributes half the donated income, see their name carried on the players' jerseys. The others have their company slogans painted on boards along the touch-lines.

Veseyans' pitch is owned in trust by their parent old boys association and of the annual playing subscription of £30 paid by their 64 players, exactly half goes to the association, which is multi-faceted. All the bar revenue goes to the association. Unless they need new goal posts, though, ground maintenance costs are negligible: there are a number of wise and willing volunteer gardeners on hand.

Travelling expenses are almost nil. The players travel to away matches in cars, usually driven by company representatives who get their petrol free. For the privilege of representing the Veseyans, the players pay £1.50 per match. They also run a monthly sweep, the 200 Club.

All of that covers the practical economics, the business part of the operation. Junior rugby, the Veseyans especially, specialises in extraneous fund-raising. Little Hardwick Lane, which is their base, houses an eccentric playwright, one David Bramble, a one-time lock forward whose annual productions are a sell-out (one of his masterpieces was to write a part for Robin Hood in the biblical epic about the crossing of the Red Sea). Their wives have legendary catering skills and special events such as gourmet evenings pack the place to the rafters. Their discos are as noisily supported as any. They are expert raffle organisers, could sell a club sweater or T-shirt to a monk and are very good at persuading vice-presidents to make an annual donation.

In short, Veseyans are as familiar with financial strain as any junior club and are as good at coping. 'The idea is not to try to make vast sums of money, is it?' asks the Club Chairman, Colin Hamilton. 'If things get a bit tight, we just have another raffle.'

FOOTNOTE: At the end of the 1990–91 season, Moseley came to the ironic conclusion that as they were about to employ a professional playing administrator, and as they had already engaged a full-time club manager, they could no longer afford Edwards' services. But the role that Edwards created is perpetuated in the commercial department that now serves all 39 of England's senior clubs. Fittingly, Edwards became its first chairman.

DAVID DUCKHAM
England Three-Quarter
1969–76

DAVID GREEN

There can have been few more glamorous players in the English game than David Duckham, the powerful Coventry and Warwickshire three-quarter who won 36 caps as both centre and wing between 1969 and 1976.

A typical Anglo-Saxon type, tall and blond, Duckham was a strong deep-chested man whose 14-stone-plus frame did not prevent him from being genuinely quick. He had a raking stride, a most deceptive swerve and sidestep and a powerful hand-off. But despite his physical appearance, he was in some ways an un-English player. Traditionally, England's selectors have tended to choose their centres less for flair, a quality which Duckham possessed in abundance, than for solidity in approach and absence of error, even though such a policy might lead to a somewhat stagnant midfield.

Gareth Edwards has shrewdly pointed out that the Welsh rugby fraternity always had a particularly soft spot for the Coventry man. The Welsh relish gifted players and because they admired Duckham's aggressive and spectacular style of play many of them referred to him as 'Dai', thereby conferring honorary Welshness upon him.

A number of Duckham's immediate predecessors in the England centre, where he first made his name, were more noted for their defensive skills than anything else, among them men like David Rosser, Terry Arthur and the unfortunate Danny Hearn, and there was certainly no obvious reluctance to shift him on to the wing. The records show that only 14 of his England caps were earned in the centre, and this despite the fact that he had early on forged a greatly respected midfield partnership with John Spencer of Headingley and Cambridge University.

The pair first played together for their country at Lansdowne Road when they were both earning their first caps, and they remained together for the next eight internationals. Of these nine matches, England won four. That

would appear a moderate performance unless England's record before 1969 is taken into account. England had won only four of their previous 19 games. Nor did matters improve after the break-up of the Duckham-Spencer partnership, for of their next 14 internationals England won only two, the first at Lansdowne Road in 1971 when Chris Wardlow partnered Spencer in the centre with Duckham on the left wing, and the second at Ellis Park in 1972 when neither toured. In the 1972 Championship season England suffered a whitewash. The pairing was only once restored during this almost barren period when England, celebrating their International Centenary, met an RFU President's XV, amounting to a world team, at Twickenham in April 1971. Unsurprisingly, England lost 28–11, but Duckham made several dazzling runs, one starting deep in his own 25.

During the ill-fated 1972 campaign, Duckham played the first three games in the centre with Bath's Mike Beese, Spencer having slipped out of the frame. Thereafter he was regarded exclusively as a wing, playing outside men like Janion, his Coventry colleagues Preece and Evans, Warfield of Northampton, and Liverpool's Dave Roughley. Though at this distance it is not easy to see what the selectors were aiming at, particularly with results continuing to disappoint, there was an argument adhered to by many that Duckham's great individual skills might be better deployed in this position, for probably his finest achievements as a player had come as a wing on the British Lions tour of New Zealand in 1971. There, despite the marvellous early form shown by the Welsh left wing John Bevan, Duckham forced his way into the Test side by the sheer brilliance of his play, displacing Bevan after the first Test and making a notable contribution to a superb series victory. It should be noted, though, that the Lions were then coached by the visionary Carwyn James and captained by John Dawes, of Wales and London Welsh, both of whom preached the importance of swift ball transfer through the three-quarters' hands and the use of the full width of the field. Not only that, they acted on the belief, and were proved correct in it, that a failed touch-kick or penalty offered a potential broken field such as pack and half-backs might work for 20 minutes to create, given regular possession.

Older rugby followers will remember the system of dummy-runs involving full-back and wings and the subsequent interplay among forwards too that this system created. No wings in the world at the time could have been better equipped to realise the potential of such a concept as Duckham and Gerald Davies, for both were masters of the arts of feint, swerve and acceleration, and both, having considerable experience in the centre, were good distributors. However, England in the 1970s did not possess the fluidity of link at half-back that Barry John and Gareth Edwards gave to the Lions and Wales, nor was their midfield play particularly deft, so the decision to play Duckham as a wing merely moved the side's most dangerous runner further away from the likelihood of receiving good ball. Thus Gerald Davies' memory of him as an opponent in England-Wales matches is of a man isolated out on the left, seldom getting a pass and therefore confined almost entirely to defensive duties.

Despite these handicaps, Duckham was always a player who opponents needed to watch carefully. Nor can he have profited from much selectorial dithering at half-back (in his eight seasons as an England player, seven fly-halves and eight scrum-halves played in a bewildering series of permutations) and centre (in his 22 games on England's wing, 13 different centres appeared, again in a variety of combinations) . . . yet he scored ten tries, a tally which puts him equal third among Englishmen.

His reputation is, deservedly, very high and might well have been a great deal higher had he played in better equipped sides. Certainly, whenever he appeared among players of true quality, as on the Lions tour or in the ever-famous match between the Barbarians and the All Blacks in 1973, his contribution was outstanding. The modesty and affability of his character (which must have been no handicap in his subsequent career in public relations) did not preclude a fierce desire to win and it must have been galling for him that during his era England found success so elusive. However, no one who watched him play, even in lost causes, is likely to forget the dash, the power or the cleverness of his running.

SELECTORS
D. Phil – the Hard Way

JOHN REASON

All the way down the years, ever since a young upstart called William Webb Ellis was given the credit for doing something that had been going on for centuries, England have always had far more young men playing football than any other country in the world. Even when the game split into different codes towards the end of the 19th century, England still had more footballers than any other country, whether they were playing the code which became known as Rugby Union, or whether they were playing any of the breakaway versions, such as Association football, Rugby League, American football or Australian rules.

That being the case, England ought to have enjoyed something like 130 years of world supremacy in all three of the versions of the football game which were developed in the British Isles. Above all, they ought to have made mincemeat of the minnows in what were then Britain's colonies who had a bit of a stab at developing Rugby Union football as their national game. However, as Magnus Magnusson persists in suggesting, a glance at the scores reveals England have done no such thing. Far from bestriding the world of Rugby Union football as the colossus of the game, England have spent most of the last century winning most of the prizes for being the game's most sporting losers.

The explanation is very simple. It is only in the last few years that England have come to terms with the notion of coaching the game at senior level, and therefore it is only in recent years that they have begun to produce men who know enough about individual skills and team construction to be able to have some hope of identifying the best 15 players in the land and assembling them in the England team. Even in the year of the 1991 World Cup, selection at the higher levels of English rugby remained in its infancy, but at least that represented an advance, because for much of the previous 100 years it was a subject about which the English had literally no conception. For most of that time, no rugby teaching whatsoever was done after a boy left school. Indeed, in many parts of the country it was held as positively impertinent to imply that anybody could so much as presume to tell an international player how he might improve his game.

This was strange because in both golf and cricket, players went on being taught and went on learning all the way through their sporting careers. Yet as late as the early 1970s, I was lectured for trying to inculcate into the national consciousness the idea that even international players could be made very much better by knowledgeable coaching. The man who gave me the lecture had been an international rugby footballer himself (admittedly of no great consequence) but he left me in no doubt that, in his view, my suggestions were worse than heresy. His tirade could be expressed in a word: 'Pshaw!' When I pointed out, in the unassertive way which is so much a part of my character, that even a professional golfer as supreme as Jack Nicklaus went back to his golf coach two or three times a year to have his swing and thinking sorted out, my face was sprayed with an even more indignant ejaculation of the same noise. When I pointed out that the logical conclusion of the argument was that only women could know anything about gynaecology, I thought the man would explode.

Fair play, though: the other countries of the world have always been quick to expess their gratitude. As Mike Gibson, masterly Irish fly-half and centre, often smilingly asserted, Ireland could always win the Triple Crown with England's left-overs. Mind you, Gibson was also the first to admit that selection in Ireland was much less of a problem because never in their history have Ireland had 15 players of genuine international standard at any one time.

'If we have nine, the team struggles,' he said. 'If we have ten, we give the other countries something to think about. If we have 11, we might sneak off with a Triple Crown. If we have 12, we might beat France as well and win the international championship. But we have never, ever, had 15.'

This means that all Ireland's selectors have ever had to do is make up the number with the best three, four or five players available. For much of their history, Scotland have been in the same boat.

England's problem has been that for most of their history they have had at least 30 players of international quality, but no one whose job it was to find them had the first idea either of who they were, or which were the best 15. So the various combinations of ancient gentlemen who had once played the game themselves and who had been asked to sit in their bowler hats and act as selectors could do no more than grope in the dark. Even as far back as 1905, when Dave Gallagher's astonishingly successful All Blacks toured the British Isles, New Zealand's rugby-wise captain said: 'All my players felt that England had a far better team available than the one that was chosen to play us.'

The All Blacks were in an excellent position to judge. They had played every county in England and had beaten them all – and England too, though organised rugby in New Zealand was scarcely 20 years old. Gallagher's book about that tour is still an educative marvel of rugby analysis, wisdom and common sense. It is also brimful of innovation about how to play the game and what is required of the players who do so. 'A back who does not have real pace,' he said, 'should find some other game to play.'

Even then, New Zealand were splitting line-outs, using coded signals, running sophisticated back moves, deliberately creating loose ball to eliminate defenders and were aware that the whole object of the game was to end up with two attackers running at one defender. It took English rugby another 65 years to learn the same lessons.

Welsh rugby was no better, even though it had a phenomenal well of talent packed into an area no bigger than 50 miles across and ten miles deep. At one stage in the 1920s Wales had 14 selectors and, in the opinion of the late Judge Rowe Harding who was then captain of Wales, not one of them had a clue. Like Ireland, though, it was easier for Wales to discern their best players because the area to be covered was so small, and the real footballing talent flowed down the valleys as naturally as the rivers to the four dominant clubs by the sea – Newport, Cardiff, Swansea and Llanelli.

In England it was much more difficult. By comparison, England was a huge country, diffuse and teeming with people, and even though the Industrial Revolution and the development of a national railway system had made the entire country accessible in a way that was far beyond New Zealand, Australia and South Africa, there were no men with the knowledge of the game and the experience to pan for rugby gold in the way that was so natural to the much more practical farming men in the colonies. When they finished playing, Englishmen finished their involvement with the dressing-room.

The waste and lack of recognition of talent in England occurred at every level, and still does. When Wavell Wakefield went up to Cambridge as already one of the most outstanding players of English rugby 70 years ago, he was appalled at what he found. So, when he was made captain of the University XV, he discarded the whole of what passed for the selection process and went round all the colleges himself, scouting for unrecognised rugby ability. He found it all over the place and drafted it into the Cambridge team, making all sorts of dramatic positional changes and changes in personnel. The bowler hats thought he was mad and Oxford started red-hot favourites to win the university match. Cambridge won by a record score, but even today, the waste of potential talent at Oxford and Cambridge is as profligate as it ever was.

In the early 1920s, when Wakefield was captain, England had one of the most successful periods in their history but still could not beat New Zealand. When the All Blacks toured the British Isles in 1924, they beat England as they beat everyone else, even though they had a man sent off the field. Since the Prince of Wales was watching at Twickenham, that event was a national disgrace for New Zealand.

SAD FACES AS THE FACT OF THE ENFORCED RETIREMENT OF (LEFT) BILL BEAUMONT IS
GLOOMILY CONTEMPLATED BY SELECTORS BUDGE ROGERS (TRACK-SUITED) AND DEREK
MORGAN

Wakefield was an innovator. Indeed, it could be argued that he did more
than anyone to develop forward play into what it has become today. He
introduced specialisation in each of the eight positions, and recognised the
distinct functions of each player in a scrummage. When he came into the
game, scrums were formed on the basis of the first forwards to arrive being
the ones to form the front row. First up, first down: Wavell Wakefield changed
all that. He also developed the concept of loose forward play, with a specialist
tearaway at open-side flank, with a specialist blind-side flanker and specialist
number 8 corner-flagging in defence and providing preplanned support in
attack. That and his organisation of defence were all new, and Rowe Harding
spent the rest of his life regretting how long it took Wales and the other home
countries to cotton on.

As a consequence of Wakefield's ideas, the physical shape, size and
capabilities of each of the eight forwards became markedly different and
more clearly defined. Instead of eight strong lumps who were all much of
a muchness, Wakefield introduced front-row forwards who were strong and
squat, a specialist hooker who was agile and had nimble footwork, and looked

56

for tall, powerful forwards who could jump and win the ball at the line-out. He also sought loose forwards who could work as a trio, any two of which could run as fast as most backs.

It was a revolutionary concept and it was a brilliant success, but again it took all eternity for the other Home Unions to recognise its merits. Indeed, just before the Second World War, England played Scotland in a match in which there was the almost unbelievable total of 96 scrums. What was even more incredible was that England won 93 of them because Scotland refused to accept that a hooker should be a specialist in the way that Bert Toft was for England. Even then, England won by only a single score.

The years after the war were not much better. One of the best forwards ever to play for England, Northampton's Don White, won 14 caps in a first-class career which lasted 15 seasons but he should have won at least twice as many. He was never chosen for a British Lions tour, either, though he certainly should have gone on two, to New Zealand in 1950 and to South Africa in 1955. Clem Thomas, who played for Wales throughout the 1950s and who captained his country, has no doubt that Don White was one of the game's finest players. Thomas was a flanker who was every bit as uncompromising as White, and he says: 'We in the Welsh team used to fall about laughing every time Don was left out of the England team. The Welsh pack of that time could always have chosen a better pack for England than the one chosen by the England selectors. Some of the non-events who were given caps by England as forwards at that time almost defied belief. Don was real class. What a player.'

The lack of understanding and the lack of basic knowledge about selection which did so much damage to Don White's international career persisted for 30 years after the war. There were occasional flashes of selectorial inspiration, such as the one that produced such a successful England team late in the period when Carston Catcheside was Chairman of the Selectors, but even he subscribed to England's traditional dogma that the whole team should be turned upside down every two or three years and youngsters brought in. They never learned, as New Zealand and South Africa did, that once a player had established himself he was always given the benefit of any doubt and went on until he had lost his own place on the field in an international match. What is more, a player like that had to be seen to have fallen from grace on more than one occasion. It worked. It provided the continuity which is so essential to successful international rugby. For England, though, it was invariably a case of 'off with the old and on with the new'. So it was that even forwards as talented as Don White and Peter Robbins were dropped long before they should have been.

The All Blacks and the Springboks knew far too much about the game to make that sort of mistake. The All Blacks in particular simply could not believe it when, in 1960, England dispensed with the services of the best fly-half that most New Zealanders could ever remember playing for a

British Lions team in their country. The fly-half in question was Bev Risman, and less than six months earlier he had finished a tour with the British Lions in which he and a wonderfully talented back division had left the All Blacks and supporters marvelling at their skill.

The following January, Risman was injured just before the match against Wales at Twickenham and had to withdraw. He was replaced by Richard Sharp, who had an outstanding game in an entirely different way after his scrum-half, Dick Jeeps, had drawn the Welsh defence by repeatedly playing the ball back inside to his loose forwards. Haydn Morgan, the Welsh open-side, had just as repeatedly sprinted to the middle of the field, where he was breathing fire and brimstone in the hope of doing the callow young Sharp a series of fearful mischiefs. Then, when Jeeps had Morgan in two or three minds about whether to run or stay at home, the England scrum-half suddenly released Sharp and let him use his scything outside break. It was a shrewd piece of football by Jeeps, and Sharp made the most of it. When, the next year, the selectors could not make up their minds between Sharp and Risman and asked Risman to play in the centre, he turned professional and went to Rugby League. Perhaps he would have done that anyway because his brother, Gus, had been among the the most celebrated of all League players, but New Zealanders who watched that Lions tour of 1959 still shake their heads that any group of selectors in their right minds could drop a footballer of the calibre of A. B. W. Risman.

The problem stemmed from a fundamental lack of knowledge among those assigned the task of choosing national teams. That knowledge was lacking because coaching at first-class club level scarcely existed and, where it did exist, was still not far removed from the drawing-board. Some bits and pieces of theory were there but not much in the way of practice. It meant that England and the other countries in the British Isles simply did not have a group of men within the game who had recently finished playing themselves and who were putting on a track-suit twice a week and going out in the wind and rain and passing on their experience to the current generation at the team practices. Had they been doing that, those men would themselves have been learning. They would have been learning about solving the problems associated with different player personalities. They would have learned about players' strengths and weaknesses, picking up wrinkles of current team play and applying that understanding. Knowledge of physical conditioning would have been expanded also. In the process, they could not have helped but learn just who were their best players and who posed the greatest threat among the teams they met. New Zealand and South Africa had always been able to take a fund of knowledge of that sort of thing for granted.

It is true that British winters are dark enough to require floodlights for practice and in those days few clubs had them, but that problem is just as acute in the South Island of New Zealand, and that never stopped South Island producing some of the best coaches in the history of the game. It didn't stop the South Africans in their primitive rural retreats on the high veldt either.

Thinking about the technology of the game began to develop in Britain in the early '60s. It was very much cat's-whisker-and-crystal-type coaching, but at least it was a start. That start was greeted with a fair amount of scepticism, but it began to fade when the lessons of the All Blacks' white-wash of the 1966 Lions sank in, a process continued when Brian Lochore's team toured England and France the following year. Coached by Fred Allen, these All Blacks went through the place like Genghis Khan. They set off with such a hiss and a roar against England that Peter Larter, one of the England locks, confessed: 'I thought they were going to score 50.'

People realised that team selection and preparation were becoming as much of a science in rugby football as in soccer. Television heightened that perception, and when the All Blacks annihilated the North of England in the first match, it persuaded an ex-Lancashire player named John Burgess that if no one else was prepared to have a go at this coaching business, he would. Several other ex-players did the same. They all realised that rugby in the British Isles had to get off its backside or go under.

Unfortunately, an abdication of 60 years cannot be repaired overnight, but British rugby was lucky in that Wales were about to go into the '70s with a spine of players who were among the best ever to play the game. Not only that, but Welsh and British rugby – though not Wales – also had the services of one of the best coaches to emerge anywhere in the world. That man was the late Carwyn James. Those players and that coach enabled British rugby to cut a good few corners in the race to catch up, but England were still slow to learn and, despite the efforts of any number of good men and true, they were dragged down by the weight of what was essentially a reactionary Rugby Union committee. This sort of thing had never been done in their day, and so on.

So it was that although the pragmatism made possible by first-hand knowledge of the nuts and bolts of playing the game was certainly making an appearance, England still showed themselves capable of making some reverberating selection mistakes. They did beat the Springboks at Twickenham on their 1969–70 tour and again at Ellis Park in 1972, as well as New Zealand at Eden Park in 1973, but two years later the wheels fell off again in terms of England selection, and so did most of the rest of the vehicle. The selectors decided that preparations for the tour of Australia should involve throwing out the whole family with the bath water. They went for youth, dispensing with the services of many of the senior players who were not only established in the England team, but who had distinguished themselves with the British Lions. England, in effect, went for broke, and broke was what they duly became.

It was a disastrous tour. Key line-out forwards like Chris Ralston and Nigel Horton were omitted, and so were men as important as Steve Smith and Alan

Old at half-back, and Peter Dixon at loose forward. Youngsters were thrown in at the deep end and, as the nearest deep end was that trench in the Pacific Ocean which is the deepest water in the world, it was scarcely surprising that some of them were never heard of again.

Even the Australians were surprised. When Garrick Fay heard what England had done, he telephoned his rugby friends in England and shared his amusement with them all; at some length. He could afford that because, despite the cost of inter-continental telephone calls in those days, Fay had made himself into something of a tycoon as well as being Australia's most successful line-out jumper.

England lost two Test matches they should have won and trailed back to London having to start the rebuilding process all over again. It is true that they were badly handicapped by injuries to players as crucial as Fran Cotton, and it is also true that their cause was not helped when Mike Burton was sent off in the first two minutes of the second Test in Brisbane, but without a core of senior players they never had a chance of developing into a team which represented the true worth of English rugby.

It was a familiar situation. The sadness was that it was created after Carwyn James and the Lions had confirmed in New Zealand in 1971 the basic tenet long held by the All Blacks and the Springboks – that if you get the senior players right in a national team, the rest of the selection process is relatively easy.

Some years before, the Rugby Football Union had published the first coaching manual produced in Europe, and Carwyn James admired both the contents of the work and the initiative which had produced it, though he did express disappointment at England's failure to find the men to implement the teachings of that manual. When James, garlanded in triumph, returned from New Zealand in 1971 to the delighted plaudits of an astonished rugby community, the Warwickshire coaching committee invited him to address one of their meetings. James said that in the normal run of things, nothing would have given him greater pleasure, but he asked, very politely, if there was any point in the exercise. He pointed out that Coventry was then the greatest club in Warwickshire, and arguably in England, but they had never had a coach and they had left no one in any doubt of their contempt for the whole concept. Twenty years on, the decline and almost the demise of this club should have left it and its fuddy-duddies in no doubt of just how utterly wrong they all were. That was their attitude at the time, though, and Carwyn James, with a twinkle in his eye, was absolutely right to twit them about it. Coventry had more ex-internationals in their bar after a club match than any other club in the land, and all of them were only too willing to tell everyone just what had been done wrong on the pitch that afternoon. The trouble was that none of them were prepared to go out on the pitch in the wet and the dark at training and try to do something about it. The club was not alone in that but, because they were so illustrious, they were the role-model for much of the country.

DON WHITE – PREMATURELY DISCARDED

Therefore, the inadequacies of the men who tried to coach and select the England team at that time were inevitable. England could only be grateful that at least a few were prepared to give up their time to try. Unfortunately, those inadequacies produced one more catastrophe as earth-shaking and as avoidable as the débâcle in Australia in 1975. This occurred in 1979. In the summer of that year, the North-Western Counties of England had combined to produce a team to tour South Africa, and the lessons learned on that tour and the experience gained enabled them to develop a solid team which looked capable of playing anybody. The players knew that they would have the chance soon because the All Blacks were due to tour the British Isles later that year, playing the North of England at Otley.

The small county ground there in Yorkshire would have been packed to the rafters even if it had been triple-decked. The match was played on the Saturday before the international against England at Twickenham, and Graham Mourie and his All Blacks knew better than anyone just what they were in for. And so it proved. The North not only beat the All Blacks fair and square, but they did it by giving probably the most disciplined, organised and talented performance in the history of English provincial rugby. You cannot argue with a score of 21–9 and four tries to one – and the All Blacks did not even get a look in.

The North had analysed the way the All Blacks had played on that tour and on the one they had made the year before, and they knew that with Fran Cotton at tight head they could beat the All Blacks in the scrums – which they did. They knew too that they could retain control of the ball in the mauls – just as long as they did not move it across field – because the All Blacks had covered their weaknesses in the tight by pressurising opposing catchers and passers and by concentrating on the business of repossession. The North were aware, therefore, that they had to keep play tight, kicking for position and driving from the scrummage to apply as much pressure close in as possible. To do that, they needed experience and kicking ability at half-back, as well as a solid defence and large quantities of common sense. Accordingly, they recalled Alan Old from near obscurity at fly-half. They chose Steve Smith at scrum-half, Roger Uttley and Peter Dixon in the back row, and shut their ears to the scoffs that they were presiding over a convention of geriatrics.

Came the day, and the old men played the All Blacks off the park. Methodically, they laid one brick on another till they had built a famous victory. Long before the end, the crowd was crowing: 'Easy! Easy!' No one could remember when, if ever, the All Blacks had suffered such an indignity.

Steve Smith, for one, was not surprised. 'When I looked round the dressing-room before the match,' he said, 'I realised that for the first time in my life, I could trust everyone who was in that team with me.'

For the international the following week, therefore, all the England selectors needed to do was make no more than the two changes which obviously would have strengthened the side. Peter Wheeler, after his success with the Lions in New Zealand in 1977, had to be chosen at hooker, and the goal-kicking of 'Dusty' Hare was needed at full-back. Nothing to it. Instead the selectors made eight changes – which led me to suggest in print that they were stark staring raving mad.

The All Blacks' mid-week match between Otley and Twickenham was at Exeter. As I walked to the ground, I saw Andy Haden, the All Blacks' celebrated lock, standing outside the gates. He looked down at me from just below the nearest cloud and said: 'Over the years, I've always thought that you've kicked the arses of the England selectors too hard. But now I know why you do it.' Andy also knew why Peter Dixon had chosen the celebrations after that smashing win at Otley as the moment to announce his retirement from the game. Dixon knew he was not going to be chosen for England. That was as tragic a mistake as England's decision not to choose Roger Uttley in their back row and to omit Alan Old at fly-half.

England trained at Leicester on the day after the match at Otley, and before they went on the field the selectors told the players what the team would be. Uttley came out early and when he trotted past me he looked across and said: 'I wish I had the courage of Peter Dixon's convictions.' I already knew that Uttley would not be in the team. So, instead of sitting back and enjoying themselves at Twickenham, watching England fashion a victory built in South Africa and in the North of England, the selectors sat on the edge of their seats watching the customary hotch-potch lose a mundane match 10–9.

For so many years England's leading players qualified to be doctors of philosophy. Each of them did it the hard way.

TONY NEARY
England Forward 1971–80

TERRY O'CONNOR

Mervyn Davies, the classic Lions number 8, confessed soon after a serious head injury cut short his playing days in 1976 that Wales were fortunate that England never fielded their best back row during his time. He held the view that his country might not have enjoyed such a successful run if faced by a back row which included Peter Dixon, Roger Uttley and Tony Neary.

Davies was well aware of the talent of these three players as he had appeared alongside them during Lions tours. In New Zealand in 1971 Dixon, an Oxford University man, was a member of the team which won the Test series 2–1 and rated one of the most knowledgeable forwards in the squad by their coach Carwyn James. Three years later on the next Lions tour, to South Africa, Uttley followed Dixon in the number 6 Test position, while Davies continued to dominate the number 8 place.

Neary was also a member of the 1974 team, but unlucky not to gain a Test place due to the presence of Irishman Fergus Slattery. Syd Millar, who coached that invincible team, admitted after selection of the first team to play South Africa that the only serious debate concerned whether to play Slattery or Neary as an open-side flanker. Slattery narrowly gained the vote because of his 1971 Lions experience and extra pace.

Even accepting the vagaries of England selection during the '70s, it is still remarkable that Uttley, Neary and Dixon never played together for their country, although two of them did feature in the same back row. The Davies view was confirmed when the three Englishmen formed the North back row which helped inflict the heaviest defeat ever suffered by an All Black team on British soil at Otley in 1979 by four tries to one. Immediately after this game, Fred Allen, the renowned All Black coach, said that on the strength of this performance his team had no chance a week later when due to meet England. I told him it was doubtful whether all the key northern players would be chosen. This proved a correct prediction as neither Dixon nor

ROGER UTTLEY IN ACTION AGAINST THE ALL BLACKS, NOVEMBER 1978

SIMON HALLIDAY IS TACKLED BY FRANCE'S PHILIPPE SELLA, MARCH 1989

PETER WINTERBOTTOM, IN ENGLAND'S CRUSHING DEFEAT OF ROMANIA IN MAY 1989

BRIAN MOORE RACES AWAY AGAINST THE IRISH AT TWICKENHAM WITH PAUL ACKFORD IN
SUPPORT, JANUARY 1990

RORY UNDERWOOD AND FRENCH FLANKER ERIC CHAMP DIVE ON THE LOOSE BALL,
FEBRUARY 1990

JEREMY GUSCOTT FINDS SPACE AGAINST THE WELSH, FEBRUARY 1990

WILL CARLING BEATS BOTH ALLEN AND TITLEY TO SCORE THE FIRST TRY AGAINST THE
WELSH, FEBRUARY 1990

FLANKER JOHN HALL EVADES THE TACKLE OF ARGENTINA'S PABLO GARRETON TO SCORE
FOR ENGLAND, NOVEMBER 1990

RORY UNDERWOOD RACES AWAY FROM THE ARGENTINIAN DEFENCE TO SCORE ANOTHER
TRY, NOVEMBER 1990

WILL CARLING IN ACTION AGAINST ARGENTINA, WATCHED BY SOME OF HIS FORWARDS,
NOVEMBER 1990

RICHARD HILL CHARGES PAST NEIL JENKINS OF WALES, JANUARY 1991

WADE DOOLEY TUSTLES FOR THE BALL AGAINST THE SCOTS, FEBRUARY 1991

ESTEVE AND DOURTHE (ON GROUND) WERE NOT GOING TO LET NEARY ESCAPE
THIS TIME

Uttley were included, nor fly-half Alan Old, in spite of a masterly display at Otley. England lost 10–9.

From 1964 onwards, when Neary won his first England cap as an under-15 schoolboy, he enjoyed a charmed rugby career. He also played for his country at under-19 level and during this period met such celebrated Welshmen on the field as J. P. R. Williams, Phil Bennett and Alan Martin, with whom he was later to tour with the Lions. By 1969 Neary was a law student at Liverpool University and a member of Broughton Park with whom he stayed at club level. Although Park were regarded as a junior club, Neary had the advantage of playing with some outstanding Lancashire teams and believes this helped him to gain international recognition. And in 1971 he won the first of 43 England caps, which stood as a record until surpassed by Rory Underwood during 1991.

John Burgess, a Lancashire coach and former President of the Rugby Union, had a major influence on Neary's early rugby thinking and approach to wing forward play. Neary developed a new concept for this position following changes in the rules. Instead of dashing all over the field tackling backs like his predecessors, he adapted to a more constructive role by keeping close to his pack, which also helped to create movements from taps from the end of line-outs, and his consistent high standard helped him to appear in every England team for six successive years.

During this period he gained the distinction of appearing in winning teams against South Africa, New Zealand and Australia within an 18-month period. The first triumph was in Johannesburg in 1972, at the climax of England's first and, into the bargain, unbeaten tour of the Republic. A year later he made a major contribution to another historic victory in Auckland.

At the end of the 1975 Championship season Neary took over as captain from his Lancashire team-mate Fran Cotton and continued as leader the following year. Then came the bombshell. He was not even included in the 1977 autumn trials. Selector Malcolm Phillips ran out of two-penny coins when telephoning to say there had been a change of thinking regarding back row tactics.

'After such a long run with England it was very disappointing as I consider I was still playing good rugby,' Neary recalls. 'I suppose I had been fortunate to hold a place for such a long period, as in those days England frequently made changes which the players did not understand. That was very much the case later, following the North's win over New Zealand in 1979.'

However, even the England selectors did not completely forget Neary, as was evident when he was called up in a crisis brought about by Mike Rafter's withdrawal through injury. The Lions selectors did not ignore Neary's many attributes as a forward either when they announced the 1977 party to tour New Zealand. As history reveals, they also named an unbalanced squad with too many Welshmen, including coach John Dawes who often appeared to show a bias towards his countrymen. During that tour Neary played some of his finest rugby but was not called up for a Test ahead of Welshman Terry Cobner until the fourth encounter with the All Blacks.

England continued to ignore Neary and he gained only one further cap, as a replacement, during the 1978 season. Eventually the selectors relented, though, and brought him back to win nine more caps – the last eclipsing John Pullin's record of 42.

It seems fitting to record a tribute from his great rival, Slattery: 'During my playing days he was easily England's finest flanker, far better on the open side than Jean-Pierre Rives of France. A complete footballer – athletic, superb support player and excellent worker with his line-out forwards.'

Looking back over the period when he gained every rugby honour possible, Neary says: 'Playing with the 1974 Lions was the most memorable experience as they were far above any other team. Also that tour helped improve my own game.' His other richest memories are being part of the 1980 Grand Slam, and of the North's unforgettable victory over the All Blacks.

COACHING AT THE TOP

ROGER UTTLEY

As a player I came into the game in the late '60s and early '70s at a time when a recognition was dawning that there was a place and a need for coaching. I grew up with the likes of John Burgess always instructing us to go 'far side, near side' at breakdowns and constantly exhorting us to 'trot' everywhere in between the action. John Elders, the Northumberland and England coach, introduced me to the basic concept of higher fitness levels and ways of attaining them. Jack Rowell, in his first successful coaching days at Gosforth, showed the importance of man-management skills and the happy knack of getting what he wanted from squads by inducing them to tell him the answers to the technical problems he would set! Then there was Syd Millar's catch-phrase with the 1974 Lions in South Africa – 'You must never go back at a set scrum.' Mike Davis was to be the most successful England coach of the '70s and '80s; video analysis was by this time creeping in, and Davis made good use of that. He was also the first coach to bring along his own overhead projector and talk us through situations on his own roll of acetate to emphasise the points he wished to make.

The fact that I can remember all these people – and there are a few more that could be added to the list – and remember clearly their individual styles and ideas is, I suggest, testament to the important role that coaches now play. But changes in our education system since the late '60s have been a further factor enhancing the importance of the coach's role – not immediately at the top level of rugby, but at grass-roots level. Coaching staffs have the power to help their clubs reach out into the local community to attract and hold youngsters in the game by presenting an appealing alternative to the other sports and recreations crowding in upon youngsters nowadays. With the pool of raw talent previously produced, by state schools in particular, now radically reduced, governing bodies of sports have had to become much more active in recruiting young players.

Coaches need more than willing helpers, however. They require a host of skills: a good telephone manner – to convince Jimmy's mum that her huge 14-year-old will be quite safe playing the game – will help, and some notion of teaching skills is desirable but most important is an idea of how skills can be developed in the game.

The 'whole, part, whole' concept is important at any level. For instance: suppose your back line cannot solve the problems involved in running and passing the ball past the opposition's defensive line. The whole problem must then be simplified into one part of it: since the essence of the problem is to create an overlap, first two men run at one, then three at two and so on, as the skill of drawing a tackler is mastered. Then, when all concerned understand their part in the exercise, the whole problem of full-back line against fully manned defence can be tackled with much greater hope of success.

Coaches need a superabundance of commitment. The players might not be too conscientious about turning up regularly – but if the coach doesn't turn up it is a disaster. And unlike the player, the coach will experience no physical relief at the end of a game. He may gain some relief if his team gains an unexpected victory – but there is nothing like playing!

With the introduction of leagues in Rugby Union in England the idea of the coach being a necessity for an aspiring club – rather than a necessary evil – has simply served to illustrate that there is a lack of good coaches in this country. Why? You might well ask. Basically, it is something of a thankless task. If the side is successful it is because you have a great team. If it is not successful, it is because you have a poor coach!

From the highest level to the lowest, the role of the coach is not greatly different and can be defined as creating and following a pattern that will achieve several things at once: skill of the individual and the team; fitness and a greater awareness of how the body works; and, perhaps most important and difficult of all, a development and understanding of how the game is played. You would be amazed at how many people think they know what is required to play the game but who in actual fact have no real concept of what is happening on the field, either as players or, worst of all, as critical spectators.

So what does it take to be a coach of Rugby Football Union in this brave new coaching-conscious world of ours? First, it is wrong to think that you must have played at a certain level to be able to coach at that same level. It is obviously beneficial if there is a good player who can turn his hand to coaching, but it certainly does not follow that to be a good coach you have to have been a good player. It can help but does not always apply. Second, the modern coach must be able to analyse matches, looking at the whole and individual performances of a team. He needs to have short-, medium- and long-term plans to which players under his charge can relate. As an example of this sort of planning one can look at the England side and the progress made in working towards the 1991 Grand Slam: since the first World Cup we had been working towards the long-term aim of winning the 1991 World Cup; medium-term goals were the yearly Five Nations Championship; short-term goals were achieving success in the

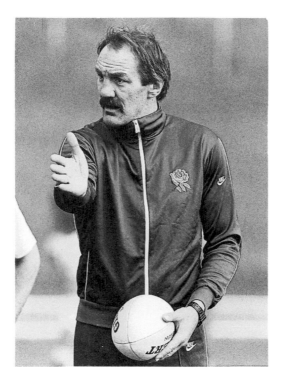

ROGER UTTLEY – 'IF THE COACH DOESN'T TURN UP IT'S A DISASTER'

individual matches and tours in between. Underpinning all the plans was a recognition that the individual levels of fitness had to be raised substantially. Players were given training schedules and targets to achieve and dates to be tested. The overall picture shortly after the 1991 Grand Slam victory was that the squad was two-thirds of the way through the specific schedules of the 18-month programme leading to the 1991 World Cup.

Over the past four years a lot of work has gone into improving both the practical skills of the individual and the groups within the team. A similar amount of work has gone into improving the players' knowledge and understanding of how to manage the events that occur during the course of a game. This is an easy thing to talk about but a very difficult area in which to become proficient. If success is to be gained it is particularly this area of work that can reap the most benefit. Will Carling's team would be one example of a band of players which is coming to terms with this aspect of the game. A player such as Rob Andrew would serve also as the classic example of an individual benefiting from the application of these ideas – taking him from being a good England player to one of true world class.

The performance of the England side in general in recent years is testament to the positive role that coaches have to play in maintaining the growth and popularity of rugby.

SIMON HALLIDAY HALTED BY VINCE CUNNINGHAM JUST SHORT OF THE IRISH LINE IN
THE 1988 MILLENIUM INTERNATIONAL, DUBLIN

IRISH VIEW
Rebuilding Pays Off

WILLIE JOHN McBRIDE

England had been threatening to record another Grand Slam since 1980. After a few near misses they collected all the prizes – Calcutta Cup, Triple Crown and Grand Slam. A tremendous effort in preparation has been achieved over three energetic years by players, coach and selectors, and in the single-mindedness and dedication of 1991 they are to be congratulated whole-heartedly.

England were elevated to the status of the country most likely to topple New Zealand in the World Cup. Now that the euphoria and emotion of the 1991 Championship are behind us it may be a useful exercise to analyse why. Let us look at how England achieved their rewards. The records show they scored 63 points from kicks and 20 from tries over the four games. The old adage must not be forgotten: 'The answer is on the scoreboard', and there's no doubt it was in England's favour on the four occasions, but a closer look at their victories game by game may prove instructive.

Wales were still in the throes of rebuilding a team after an abnormally heavy loss of players, particularly to the professional code. England did a demolition job at Cardiff against a side of little experience – but then so did everyone else. Ireland should also have won at Cardiff with almost a new side, and only inexperience let them down – but they still managed four tries.

In the Scottish game there was little between the teams except that Scotland gave away an unusual number of penalties and Simon Hodgkinson had a field day.

Against Ireland, England were a beaten team for 70 minutes, and again inexperience allowed the match to slip in England's favour in the last ten minutes. I find it remarkable to recall that England periodically piled tremendous pressure on the Irish line that day and the new Irish pack repelled the danger again and again.

France are always an unknown quantity and, while England won, France

71

still looked the more dangerous and confident team, willing to show off their skills. Only the French can play that way, and the memory of the movement which brought Saint-André's try lingers – surely this was close to perfection! Again, France scored three tries to England's one.

To my way of thinking, this makes for all manner of reservations about England's position. We are told that Carling's team are the best balanced England blend for years. Why then did they employ the hard-driving ten-man game with Rob Andrew controlling? Surely Carling and Guscott are confident players and surely Underwood is one of the best wings ever to play for England? How can he become a world's best if he is not given the ball? It has often been said that All Black rugby can become boring with their relentless forward play – but they score tries.

I have the greatest respect for Roger Uttley but he must be aware that this England pack, now averaging into the 30-year-old mark, have been stretched at times over the tough Championship they won, and 30-year-olds don't recover as quickly as is sometimes necessary.

England invented the game and have always been difficult to master over the years – certainly that has been the case for Ireland. Indeed, recent years have definitely brought tremendous change for the better for England: the introduction of the Leagues and the grading of players towards the First Division have certainly meant improved selection. This has helped to build a confidence in the English team not evident in earlier years. Gone are the days when an Englishman's aim was to get his 'cap' and be satisfied. Now they want to be part of a successful team and not disappear for ever to the has-beens' bench with their one, two or three caps.

The old divide between north and south now also appears to be easing with the uniform structure in the coaching set-up. This too can only be good for England. It has also been said that if England are strong then the four countries are strong because we all want to beat them – long may that attitude continue. Probably the main strength of the English is that they believe they are best, and the rest of us sometimes prove them wrong.

It has also been said that individually and collectively Carling's side is England's best to date. Individually, I do not agree. Players over my span of years who really would rank the best of English talent are Wheeler, Pullin, Cotton, Neary, Uttley, John Currie, Beaumont, Scott, Jeeps, Steve Smith, Richard Sharp, Duckham and Peter Jackson – not to mention Hiller and Hare. Surely all these are world-class – men with whom I have had many memorable battles and, most of all, memorable Lions tours.

None were better in 1974 than Cotton, Neary and Uttley. I look upon Duckham as the best wing to play for England, and Richard Sharp as the most complete outside-half. 'Dusty' Hare and Bob Hiller had few peers at full-back, and John Pullin doubled as hooker and captain superbly. If the abovementioned had enjoyed the same preparations as present-day players, surely England would have been world beaters.

DUSTY HARE – HERE SLIPPING TACKLES IN AN ENGLAND TRIAL – IS THE McBRIDE CHOICE
AS NUMBER ONE AT FULL-BACK

This is my choice of a composite side from my observations of England down the years:

HARE

DUCKHAM   CARLING   GUSCOTT   UNDERWOOD R.

SHARP   HILL

RENDALL   PULLIN   COTTON (OR PROBYN)

CURRIE   ACKFORD

NEARY   RICHARDS   UTTLEY

So how does an Irishman sum up the English? The story has been told concerning the prominent English lock who was floored by Colin Meads. Returning to the perpendicular, he shook the New Zealander's hand. When asked why he reacted in this manner, he replied: 'I just wanted to make him feel a cad.' But those days have gone. The English now know how to win and they have proved it. Which means that we, the Irish, will continue to hold that our finest hour is when we beat England at Twickenham.

England's record against Ireland
P104 W60 D8 L36

JEFF BUTTERFIELD
England Centre 1953–59

TERRY O'CONNOR

Jeff Butterfield was ahead of his time regarding fitness and the need for team organisation. At the time he joined the England team in 1953, most of his colleagues regarded rugby as a weekend game requiring the occasional run apart from club training. Butterfield, a physical education teacher from Loughborough College, trained every day and even then argued for England to hold squad sessions.

His pleas were in vain. Any form of coaching was then regarded as professional; international selection was haphazard and depended on form shown in often meaningless trials. Teams from the British Isles only assembled on the Friday afternoon before an international. At least this provided an opportunity for some to meet for the first time. It was not until the late '60s that coaching and the need to organise teams became accepted. It still took another 20 years before rugby caught up with other sports like athletics and swimming where a scientific approach had been adopted to cope with rising standards worldwide.

Cliff Morgan, who had the advantage of playing for the efficient Cardiff club, considers Butterfield made a major contribution to the success of the 1955 Lions in South Africa. It was not just his skill in creating tries as a centre, but his ability to organise the team training.

'There was a tremendous amount of individual talent in the party, but in those days a coach was not appointed,' says Morgan. 'Therefore, we were fortunate to have Butterfield. He was not only the fittest member of the team but he also had a marvellous tactical brain. This, combined with his background as a physical education teacher, helped him to take training and develop a unified team approach.

'Buttercups was a well-balanced runner and beautiful passer of the ball which provided extra room for the wings to score tries. Given the opportunity he could score himself as he was exceptionally fast. I remember giving him the ball only 30 yards from our line and he ran more than 70 yards before selling a dummy and going under the posts. Even that speedy wing Tom van Vollenhoven, who later became a Rugby League star, could not catch him. In one match against Orange Free State he scored three tries to make a major contribution to a handsome victory. Next day a headline in the *Rand Daily Mail* read: "Not Murrayfield, but now it is Butterfield". That was a reference to the game against Scotland four years earlier when the Springboks won 44–0.'

Butterfield played in all four Tests during a 2–2 drawn series with some outstanding backs like Dickie Jeeps, Morgan, W. P. C. Davies, Tony O'Reilly and Gareth Griffiths – apart from forwards like Courtney Meredith, Bryn Meredith, Stoker Williams, Rhys Williams and Jimmy Greenwood.

Born in August 1929, Yorkshireman Butterfield admitted that he gained much of his early rugby knowledge watching Bradford Northern Rugby League Club during and after the war. One of the stars of that team was Willie Davies, a pre-war Welsh international outside-half.

'Willie always carried the ball with both hands in front of him and continued to run straight when he passed. I modelled my game on Willie's technique but discovered when I joined Northampton that I did not kick well enough to be considered as a first-class outside-half. One of the main faults with modern three-quarters is that they move towards a colleague when about to pass and this makes it easier for the defence. The secret is to receive and pass without changing direction which forces opponents to be committed.'

When Butterfield first went to Loughborough in 1946 he believed his best chance of sporting success was as a swimmer, but soon discovered he did not have the necessary pace. As a Cleckheaton player he found it difficult to find a place even in the second team because of the presence of so many mature players returning from war service. After two years with the army on national service, during which he played with the England half-backs Denis Shuttleworth and Mike Harding, he returned to Loughborough to take a diploma. A teaching post at Wellingborough G.S. followed which was fortunate as it took him to Northampton, a club then in the process of developing one of the finest teams in England. Here he joined stars like Louis Cannell, John Hyde, Chalky White, Dickie Jeeps and Ron Jacobs.

Playing in such celebrated company against the best clubs in England and Wales helped Butterfield gain early recognition. In 1953 he replaced Albert Agar in the match against France and made an instant impact. After only a minute Butterfield pounced on a mistake by outside-half Haget to make a long run before creating a try for Ted Woodward. Near the end he crowned a successful début by scoring a try.

Looking back on an England career which included 28 caps between 1953–59, Butterfield's highlight was the match against Australia in 1958 at Twickenham, won by a superb Peter Jackson try in the 14th minute of injury time. It was a bruising encounter with numerous injuries, especially on the England side. Ten minutes before half-time Philip Horrocks-Taylor went off, forcing Butterfield to play at outside-half. Next Butterfield was carried off on a stretcher. He recovered quickly and returned to the field. This was also the game where booing was heard at Twickenham for the first time after Australian centre Jim Lenehan kicked wing Peter Thompson.

'Jackson's winning try was unforgettable,' said Butterfield. 'It not only produced a fantastic climax, but it was magnificently executed. John Currie started the move, winning a line-out 25 yards from the Australian line. Like a flash, Jeeps passed to me. A rapid exchange between Malcolm Phillips and John Robbins, a flanker playing centre, gave Jackson the ball 15 yards from the touch-line and room to operate. He weaved and dodged to beat four defenders before touching down. That try illustrated the importance of being able to catch and pass quickly.'

The next season, when Butterfield was selected as captain, proved to be his last with England. It was a major disappointment for him as England failed to score a try and only beat Ireland by a penalty goal to nil with draws against France and Scotland. Later that year he was included in the Lions party but Butterfield's best rugby was played, in his opinion, on the tour of South Africa. He loved running on the ground of the high veldt rather than the soft pitches in Britain because it gave him more time to exploit his particular skills. Similarly, W. P. C. Davies enjoyed receiving perfect passes as this allowed him to make ground with his power running.

Following his active rugby days, Butterfield played a prominent role in the preparation of the Rugby Football Union coaching manual during the early '60s which was the first ever produced by a home Union. He served for three years as an England selector and is now proprietor of the Rugby Club of London, Hallam Street, near Oxford Circus, which has 6,000 members and organises world-wide rugby supporters' tours.

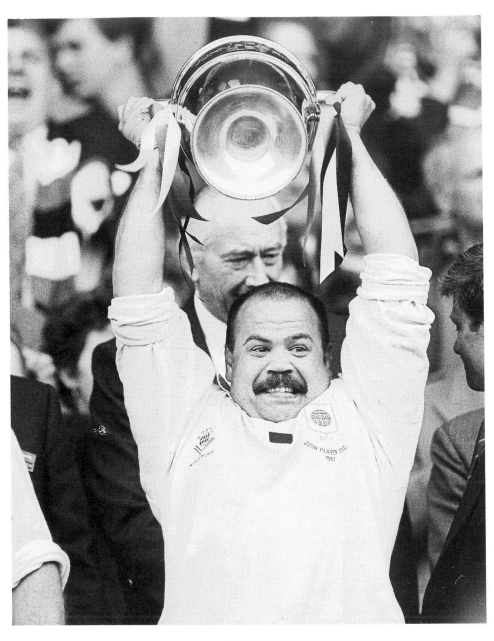

GARETH CHILCOTT, WHO PLAYED A FULL PART AS BATH GOT THE HANG OF LEAGUE
WARFARE

THE LEAGUES
Home and Away is on the Way

TERRY COOPER

There has probably never been such a widespread and fundamental revolution in the structure of a major sport as that which took place in September 1987, when 1,200 English Rugby Union clubs began playing League matches.

Perhaps the mingling of professional and amateur lawn tennis players in 1968 – they all soon began playing for money – is a comparable change. But that affected no more than a few hundred players. In the Courage Clubs Championship about 18,000 players compete for League points ten times a season. Too many defeats in this eventually mean that clubs accustomed to appearing in large arenas are condemned to slumming it on council park pitches. For the teams that really fancy themselves, and match their self-esteem by winning, there is the ultimate goal of playing at Leicester, Bath or Gloucester.

London Welsh are the prime example of a glamorous team falling on hard times – relegated in successive seasons from both Division Two and Division Three. But they are not moaning about playing against the likes of Maidstone and Southend within 15 years or so of being capable of filling every club stadium in Wales. They are determined to sort out the methods which no longer work and drag themselves back to respectability.

Teams who have seized avidly on the chance of improvement include, remarkably, four who achieved promotion in all the first three seasons. Even more remarkable is that two of them are from Romford, in Essex – Old Edwardians and Campion. The other two are Veseyans, from Sutton Coldfield, and Sheffield Oaks. For them to challenge the traditional majors is their dream of an ideal world. So far there has not been enough time for any side to mount a promotion-parade that leads from backwater to the First Division, and there will be many who find the drawbridge insurmountable when they reach fortresses in the uplands of the National Divisions, North or South. Still, the possibility does exist, whereas the mountain was not there to climb before 1987. Fixture secretaries picked and chose who they played and if Harlequins could disregard Wasps or Saracens in the not-too-distant past (which they did) what chance did somebody outside the magic circle have of competing against the cream, except for the fleeting miracle of a long Cup run?

The Leagues have been with us for four seasons and the overwhelming response from the players, officials and spectators is that they have galvanised the game just when its morale was much in need of radical improvement. There has been some grim rugby; there has been some defensive rugby; there has certainly been plenty of kicking, and penalty goals have dominated countless contests. But there were desperately dull games in the old days – meaning any year up to 1986 – when the result did not matter beyond the second jug of beer that Saturday night. Now if a game contains limited skill or ambition, no suggestion of a try, with the goal-kickers playing aerial ping-pong against each other, the outcome still matters to the participants and supporters. With all but the top three Divisions each consisting of 11 clubs or fewer, even teams apparently locked in mid-table can become interested in promotion after stringing together a couple of winter wins, or anxious about relegation following a poor trot.

Fears that violence would increase have been largely unfounded. The game has become harder as the players have become fitter, but it has not become dirtier. Even the dimmest forward soon appreciated that his team's results would take on a care-worn look if he persistently got himself sent off or conceded a string of penalties for kicking or punching. However, there has probably been an increase in the cynical, or what some call 'technical', offence – killing the ball at a ruck or simple offside in a defensive position. The defenders are willing to trade off the possibility of three penalty points conceded against the likelihood of four (maybe six) for the try. Sooner or later some brave referee is going to enter unknown territory by sending off somebody for persistent infringement, even though the offences are non-violent.

Bill Bishop, the genial Cornish Chairman of the Competitions Committee of the Rugby Union who, with his fellow toilers on that Committee, set up the whole edifice in 1987, is justifiably proud of what is already part of the furniture.

'Nobody has been against the principle. Of course, there have been endless issues, large and small, to settle. The junior clubs say we look after the senior clubs: the senior clubs are eager to safeguard their status: and the counties argue about the structure. But the principle is accepted,' Bishop emphasises.

'The request came from the grass-roots. There was no question of the top clubs imposing competitive rugby on the juniors. In fact, some seniors had intimations that what has happened to London Welsh might have happened to them – and still might.

'Those who wanted to join did so and those who wanted to continue playing friendly fixtures from September to April carried on doing so, though there are strictly limited fixtures available to them on our League days. There are several hundred clubs not involved in the Leagues. Many of them, by their definition, find it impossible to commit themselves to regular, defined Saturday fixtures. I mean Forces teams, police and fire-service clubs, universities, colleges and polytechnics, midweek sides and others who cater for the irregular or casual player. Think of the Barbarians.

'And don't forget that any player who does not relish the idea of the stress that competition can impose is able to obtain relaxed rugby in his second or third XV. No club has more than one team playing League rugby. Since most clubs run a couple of teams below their first XV the bulk of rugby played each League weekend is non-competitive. We satisfied a universal demand for the sharp edge of competition without taking away the traditional, unregimented nature of the game as we knew it for the ordinary player. We are not euphoric, but we are convinced that the plus points heavily outweigh the minus factors.

'The clubs are having to get switched on to the needs of financing on an organised basis and the pin-pointing of the League weekends enables an enterprising outfit to attract sponsors. It's all a bit more business-like than collecting a few bob in match-fees in the bar after the game.

'They are also having to become switched on to the need for coaching. It's inconceivable that a set-up that disregards the importance of good coaching can succeed.

'Some clubs have not adapted, but those that were buzzing and had a forward-looking mentality have continued to thrive. The good have got better and the bad have got worse. But there is still hope for those who have sunk from the position they held in the mid-1980s and have had a depressing time in recent seasons. They should bottom-out and start winning when they find their true playing level.

'It's extraordinary to think that top clubs were concerned about the Anglo-Welsh fixtures that were rated highlights of the season and big money-earners. Now they don't mean a thing compared with that top-of-the-table clash against a team from another part of the country that had not been heard of locally until the two sides were linked in the same Division,' says Bishop.

Eric Smith, the northern mastermind of the League concept who compiled both the rejected blueprints for a League structure in 1975 after the Mallaby Report and in 1981 after the Burgess Report, makes a similar point.

'The local fixtures that went back into the last century, in which old rivals hammered away at each other twice a season, are vanishing, and where they still exist they don't matter a damn.'

This is one of two aspects that concern Smith and which the administrators are going to watch closely. 'I am not sure whether we are being taken away from the amateur ethos of the game. I would hate it if it went semi-pro.'

On the issue of non-League fixtures, Smith says: 'I would use all these spare Saturdays to introduce home and away in the Leagues as soon as possible. I'm afraid that the Leagues have cast a blight over other games.'

Don Rutherford, Technical Director of the Rugby Union, also sees a problem with those spare weekends, knowing that regular spectators feel slightly cheated and disillusioned when a pick-'n'-mix side, composed of first-, second-, and third-XV players, turns out in a fixture that used to be special.

'But it does give the second-team player an opportunity to perform alongside those first-teamers who do appear. That can only be good when it comes to them being selected for the main squad.

'From the point of view of international players, Leagues have made life simpler and most are achieving the amount of match-play that we thought they would never reduce to. Some time ago we identified no more than 30 games as about right for the England squad. But some continued to push through the 40 mark. Now they play their 12 League matches, internationals, Divisional and Cup-ties and the friendly games that they deem necessary for their own practice and fitness needs. The result should be under 30 matches, but the total may start hovering around the 30 mark when – not if – we have home and away. The size of the Divisions will be reduced for home and away, but there must be more League games.

'That remains to be sorted out, but what I am convinced of is that there has been a link with England's recent international successes and the introduction of Leagues. OK, many of the current squad like Rory Underwood, Rob Andrew and Peter Winterbottom were established internationals at the start of the 1987 season. But some, like Jason Leonard, know nothing except a season based on competitive action. All players coming through know what is required and selection becomes more straightforward when you can watch the best against the best almost whenever you like,' adds Rutherford, whose responsibility for improved skill at all levels includes the England XV.

Leonard's swift switch from Saracens to Harlequins immediately after he had become a Test player on the tour of Argentina in 1990 raised the question that can be guaranteed to provoke the offended club to frenzy: was he on the end of a nod and a wink which said: 'You'll be all right with us'? In Leonard's case, it made sense for him to do his best to secure his potentially prolonged international future by going to play alongside Harlequins' batch of internationals. By propping England's hooker, Brian Moore, and being shoved by Paul Ackford and Peter Winterbottom, Leonard was profiting from playing in the same scrum as the acknowledged best. A straight rugby decision.

But Michael Pearey, President of the Rugby Union, felt bound to warn in the *Courage Directory*, the publication of which coincided with Leonard's 'transfer': 'There are, of course, dangers in such a competitive structure, principal among them being the temptation for clubs to attract players of repute by improper inducements. The RFU will have no hesitation in calling to account clubs where this is perceived to be happening.'

Finally, there's the view of the players – from Peter Winterbottom, the longest-serving member of England's Grand Slam team, who has graduated from local, friendly rugby with Headingley in Yorkshire to captaining Harlequins, team of all the talents.

'The game has altered beyond all recognition, but there is no doubt that from the late 1970s there was a desire among players for more competition. Winning and losing and results mattering were increasingly becoming objectives. But officials at the time simply could not take in the concept and we thought that what we have now would always be unobtainable.

'Very fortunately there was the halfway house of the Merit Tables, which were based on existing fixtures and so caused no disturbance to old friends meeting on the same Saturday every year. But they tell me that Harlequins' unusual fixture list, with so many Welsh clubs, the Services and the universities, allowed them to play only four Merit Table games in some seasons, and even when the tables were status-related [Tables A and B] they actually played only two Merit matches in the final season of that system.'

Winterbottom is right, and both Orrell and Wasps participated only twice, as against other clubs' six or seven fixtures. There were rows about 'de-meritising' – now an obsolete word – and clearly such nonsense could not continue. Perhaps, because it was so farcical, the real thing came about more speedily. Even in the first League season, 1987–88, the games were scattered all over the autumn, winter and spring, and some teams did not bother to complete their full list. Leicester won the First Division.

'Things fell into place when we had the structured season of fixed League Saturdays for 1988,' says Bill Bishop. Bath were the second winners and Wasps completed a hattrick of famous names taking the trophy. This situation will not change much, and then only gradually, but look what ten years can do. Here is Eric Smith's still-born prototype for Leagues in 1981:

DIVISION ONE: Bristol, Gloucester, Gosforth, Leicester, Moseley, Orrell, Rosslyn Park, Wasps, Waterloo

DIVISION TWO: Bath, Bedford, Coventry, Fylde, Harlequins, Liverpool, London Scottish, London Irish, Richmond

DIVISION THREE: Blackheath, Broughton Park, Exeter, London Welsh, Northampton, Nottingham, Roundhay, Sale, Wakefield

BOB HILLER
England Full-Back
1968–72

JOHN MASON

There is a splendid tale about Bob Hiller, who deftly walked the tight-rope stretching between intense competition and rollicking humour at the time he was about to become a double Blue (rugby and cricket) at Oxford. It goes something like this:

Hiller:	If I get into the XI, presumably there'll be an entry in *Wisden*?
Captain (Richard Gilliat):	Yes.
Hiller:	That could be a problem.
Captain:	Why?
Hiller:	I've only got one initial.
Captain:	I beg your pardon.
Hiller:	I can't possibly go into *Wisden*, the cricketer's bible, with one initial. From now on I'm R. B. Hiller – 'R' as in Robert, 'B' as in Bob.
Captain:	Initially speaking . . .

Alas, the story is apocryphal '. . . very much Old Testament,' adds Hiller, with the straightest of faces. 'Apocryphal? It's not true either.'

But it *is* true, I am delighted to record, as far as *Wisden* is concerned. At random, I selected the 1974 annual from my shelves: there on page 1046, right-hand column, line 19, between 'W. A. Hill (Warwicks) b. April 27, 1910' and 'H. M. Hills (Essex) b. Sept 28, 1886' is the entry – 'R. B. Hiller (Oxford Univ) b. Oct 14, 1942'. A cross-reference, page 775, as one would expect of *Wisden*, confirms the detail.

The authorised version relates, in any event, to rugby, a sport in which

BOB HILLER PUTS ONE OVER FOR SURREY AGAINST MIDDLESEX

Robert Hiller, from Bec School, Tooting, and erstwhile member of Mitcham Cricket Club, played 19 matches for England, including seven as captain, and scored 138 points, a national record which stood for more than a decade. He also toured with the British Lions in 1968 (South Africa) and 1971 (New Zealand), scoring more than 100 points over the two trips, without getting into the first-choice side. Tom Kiernan and a certain J. P. R. Williams played in all eight Tests on those tours.

At about the time Hiller, a civil engineering student at Birmingham University and a post-graduate at Oxford where he took a Diploma in Education ('It was all McPartlin's fault'), was beginning to make a mark in the senior game, another goal-kicking full-back was also winning semi-national attention – Russ Hillier, who played for Stroud and Gloucestershire.

Hiller, a devoted Harlequin, explains: 'He was R. J. Hillier, and in next to no time the newspapers, bless 'em, had put two and two together . . . and confusion reigned. What with other misspellings, you work out the permutations.

'Whatever they might be, over a surname with one letter different and a christian name with the same initial letter, they came up. Needless to say, when I played badly, I claimed it was Russell. I think I must have damaged his career . . .

'I was often listed as R. J. Hiller and, in due course, presumably because of a telephone mis-hearing somewhere one afternoon, that became R. B. Hiller, which was the one which stuck. By the time I'd finished, I think I was back to one initial. But you can't win.

'When I returned to teaching in Wimbledon, it was the K.C.S. custom for common-room lists and the like to denote the staff by their initials. I instantly became R. B. H. again – and still am.'

It would be very wrong, though, to regard Hiller only as a gifted sportsman whose sense of the ridiculous, linked to an agile brain able to prick the pompous, could cause anything from a wry smile to a belly laugh. On the one hand, here is the immensely talented all-rounder, summer and winter – Oxford's opening bowler in 1966 at Lord's (four wickets, three catches) who shared in an innings victory and within 18 months was England's full-back against Wales at Twickenham.

'When Gilliat saw I was next to bat, he declared,' says Hiller in a bland dismissal of his cricketing activities. 'I attended Surrey nets at The Oval and played for Mitcham for a while. But I'll let you into a secret – I wasn't good enough.'

On the other hand, wearing the winter hat, here is the tactician, the technocrat, the analyst, the intense competitor who abhorred defeat – and a supreme goal-kicker whose sustained accuracy set the standards in England for Dusty Hare and Simon Hodgkinson. At a time when England's indifferent record did not stand too close an examination, Hiller won matches for his country that otherwise would have been lost. Misery was put on hold for a fraction longer, he told me once. Such intensity needed a safety-valve and in that respect, like the quality of mercy, our man has been twice blessed.

Humour, though, has been only one weapon in a sporting crusade in which battle has been waged anywhere from the lofty portals of the Twickenham temple to a fourth-team pitch somewhere off the Kingston By-pass, down the lane, third turning on the right, change behind the hedge. And there is something else called personality, the ability to exude a cheerful confidence which, in Hiller's case, is disturbed only by slackness or a dragging of the feet.

International and Harlequin first-team selection stopped, but Hiller did not. Rugby's grass-roots ('Well, weeds really') enjoyed his whole-hearted services for ten years and more. A new range of opponents, the long, the short and the tall, the good, the bad and the ugly, discovered that England's former captain talked a lot and still did not like losing, could kick goals almost as well as ever and, if necessary, still possessed a conveniently broken bootlace ('Well, hamstring occasionally') when the large opposition number 8 was bearing down on his try-line at a rate of knots.

At the last time of asking, the playing had ceased ('I want to go to work on Mondays') but training had not. Nor had selection duties with Quins, responsibilities which, several times over, England would dearly have liked him to take up. The polite refusal was less a reluctance to be involved than the belief that he did not have the time required for the job to be done properly. There have been sundry approaches through the years, notably from Budge Rogers when Chairman of Selectors, but Hiller has remained adamant.

He shudders at the thought of being labelled a perfectionist. Yet countless friends will insist that, deep down, that is what he is. High standards of performance and behaviour have been the shining beacons in a sporting life in which Bob Hiller – never R. B. Hiller – who has had more than his share of disappointments, has, initially speaking, masked his feelings with a smile: 'Well, no one could tell the difference. It was my gum-shield really.'

CHALKIE WHITE, 'DOING THINGS LEICESTER'S WAY'

COACHING THE CLUBS

CHALKIE WHITE

My charting of the progress of coaching in English rugby is a decidedly subjective exercise, as my experience, my contact with the game and my opinions are not typical. In many ways, what I had seen and what I had done before arriving at Leicester late in 1957 had not prepared me for the culture shock at the Aylestone Road ground. The ground itself sets the club apart, but undoubtedly the most significant factor is the long tradition of doing things Leicester's way. In common with the practice at all other clubs, captains were responsible for what passed as team preparation. Previous captains had or had not left their mark.

One of them, a short and relatively slight forward, Colin Martin from New Zealand, was the most influential player in those early days. In a word, he 'understood' aspects of the game that elsewhere were barely recognised as crucial constituent parts of the game. Admittedly, most of his understanding revolved around forward play, but he brought to this a purpose that was as universal in New Zealand as the grass they play on. Thirty years later that 'understanding' is not yet common throughout the game in England, but enormous strides have been made. Young and not so young players are being introduced to the undisputed facts of good play.

As an elected member of the Leicester Football Club Committee, I was asked to help with training by the then captain, David Matthews, a situation definitely not universally approved. Fellow committee members were surprised: 'He spends far too much time with the players!' Senior players had no liking for being asked to change their ways. For them, a pattern would be: training night(s) . . . but no training programme; the matches . . . all friendlies in England; the social thing . . . extremely important, including an acknowledgment of the opposition. A very fair number talked rugby, a much smaller number did not. Those involved in the game were nice guys and conspicuously content most of the time . . . not the breeding ground for change.

Also, the attitude of a succession of captains to a change of such arrangements varied from one extreme to the other. Persistence and some fortitude were called for with the introduction of changes as progress was made.

In August 1969 Albert Agar and Don White assembled a group of players for what was probably the first ever 'England practice session'. Change was under way. A succession of captains of the national side continued to instigate other developments and Bob Hiller and Dick Greenwood, as a player and as a coach, played notable parts in the progression. The national coaches all continued this, but it must be said that the outstanding managerial and organisational skills of the first honorary team manager, Geoff Cooke, with the response he has received from the players and others around him, have moved the game forward in England at a pace never before experienced.

Geoff Cooke's remarks when in Argentina near the end of a difficult and not entirely successful tour were much nearer the root of the problem than perhaps he made clear. The majority of player development work is done in the clubs. Representative teams at the highest level are scratch sides, and until recently many were drawn together without too clear an idea of how they were to win after a very small number of training sessions together. The forward-thinking clubs will produce training programmes that are tailor-made for individuals as well as for the teams within the clubs. There will possibly be 80 training sessions each season to achieve what they set out to do. Questions must be asked. How much more competent is the player who attends all his club training nights? In the forward-looking club an out-of-season fitness training programme will be available, so that players arrive at a higher level of fitness each year they play. Gone are the days when a player started each season at the same uncertain level of fitness.

As levels of fitness improve so must levels of technical competence. Each year will show some progress built on the experience of the previous season. Unfortunately, not very long ago there was no particularly obvious incentive for clubs to provide development plans for their players – in spite of the outstanding efforts of the RFU Technical Administrator, Don Rutherford, and the coaching structure he provided. Much of what was done was carried out in a vacuum. However, two highly significant events did force radical changes on rugby in England.

First, the advent of the World Cup focused attention at national level, despite fairly substantial and misplaced opposition initially, for the rather cosy Five Nations Championship, which ensured two sell-out home games each season regardless of previous seasons' results, now assumed greater significance. World Cup seeding was at stake! Teams round the rim of the Pacific were now keen to have a bit of the action.

Before this, coaches and players looked to the Lions tours as being likely to provide some kind of impetus to the development of playing ideas and techniques. Sad to say, on only one occasion in the last 25 years have the Lions provided the domestic game with a lead. The 1971 Lions tour to New

Zealand gave an example of what the emerging wave of coaches and players could copy or develop for their own use. The success in 1974 in South Africa could have made a point, somewhat negative perhaps, but the opportunity was not taken. The lower levels of attainment in 1980 and 1983 brought the realisation that a rethink was necessary.

Secondly, attention was focused upon coaching requirements at club level by the introduction of a League structure in England. The difficult task of the RFU Competition Sub-committee has possibly been complicated by trying to accommodate too many factors. They have not yet produced an ideal structure, but an evolutionary process is discernible and ultimately clubs and players will benefit – to the extent that good players will have to play well more often, and their clubs will help them to do so.

It would be comforting to think that all clubs in the top divisions of the League could progress as well as, say, Orrell, where rugby manager Des Seabrook is operating in a club environment that takes advantage of all its assets and realistically faces all its problems. John Burgess showed the way forward here some years ago for Lancashire; Orrell have taken over as the trend-setters for the north, while Bath have their sights set on worthwhile and worldwide targets. How difficult it is to reach those targets without a single-mindedness throughout the club is obvious. Nevertheless, examples of this clarity and unity of purpose are not only to be drawn from clubs. Students at Loughborough were introduced to significantly higher standards of play by John Robins and Jim Greenwood, and students at St Luke's College, Exeter, were exposed to similar beneficial influences.

The clamorous demands of club playing-structure often prove a difficult challenge when some of these players abandon student status. There are clubs who have been slow to recognise that the development of young players has to be a continuous process and one that is achieved, not by the simple expedient of offering them more games per season than is physically good for them, but by introducing them to training programmes, skill drills and technical training, as well as enlightened fitness programmes. Indeed, the national fitness advisers, especially Rex Hazeldine, have made the unpleasant, sweaty business of getting fit much more meaningful in a way that is comparatively attractive. Those clubs who have accepted their responsibilities are planning ahead. Player development is recognised as being crucially important. Good players are a club's most valuable resource; they have to be nurtured. Clubs with technical directors will, together with the club coach, ensure that the training sessions throughout the season lead the club in general and the players in particular as individuals in the right direction.

The divisional programme has produced a difficult testing ground for both players and coaches. Lessons made available from these games are no more easy to digest than were previous victories by the North, the West Midlands and the Midlands against New Zealand and Australia. Likewise the halcyon days of the 1920s produced no English style of play any more than the Triple

Crown years of the 1970s did for Wales or success in the Five Nations Championship did for France. But some learning is taking place. Many players now have an understanding of how the game can best be played and there is a much greater awareness of the importance of development work at an earlier stage in their playing careers.

The National Young Players' Week, with more than 200 of the best boys in attendance each year, gives them an insight into what is necessary to play the game well. Indeed, the RFU's appointment of 30 youth development officers will increase the awareness in clubs of the necessity to provide good coaching and viable development programmes for players, especially at an early age. The success of the national side is a fillip for club coaches helping aspiring players. The initiative shown by the Divisions to substantiate their role in development by producing Divisional 'B' and under-21 teams has provided emerging players with clear incentives. But above all it will be the training programmes *within* clubs, supported by sound administration behind the scenes, that will continue the on-field progress made in recent years. Vast improvements in ball retention and continuity skills, allied to realistic fitness programmes, will be the hallmark of successful League clubs. Reputations will count for nothing.

Progress achieved by ambitious clubs is now readily discernible. The London clubs have an advantage in the present economic climate. Midland clubs, where Alan Davies has set very high standards at Nottingham, have reacted to present-day problems while Northern clubs, the shining example of Orrell apart, have been slow in catching up, though they are now realising that simply being in a League does them no favours. Clubs at the top of the various sections do not tow the lower clubs along. Those at the bottom lose touch rapidly as promoted clubs overtake them. Yet there is no more chastening experience than for a promoted club to be relegated the following season.

Player production – the end that can be accomplished by means of competent club organisation, financing and coaching expertise – is the way ahead: the large number of skilful players at Bath did not happen by accident. Nor did the advances being made by many so-called junior clubs. Their ability to promote themselves as a community amenity catering for a wide range of ages, abilities and interests bodes well for the future. Having to move rapidly on to more taxing levels of performance by their adept young players may not be a comfortable way forward, but further development demands a stronger challenge in the company of players of at least comparable ability. More purposeful change must come to build on progress made in recent years and make continued advance of benefit to all – and understood by all.

DICKIE JEEPS
England Scrum-Half
1956–62

TERRY COOPER

Dickie Jeeps had to wait until he was 24 years old for his first England cap. He made up for this inconvenience by achieving almost everything else in his sporting and public life many years, even decades, earlier than normal. He was a Test British Lion before he had worn England's shirt; on the Rugby Union Committee at 30; and President of the Union at 44 – only a couple of presidents this century have been younger; while away from rugby he was a local councillor – 'Independent – I polled more than the rest put together' – JP at 28, and Chairman of the Sports Council at 46.

He became England captain in 1960. As in 1991, England went through the Championship unchanged – 'and *we* would have won the Grand Slam but for Don Rutherford hitting the post with a conversion in Paris when we drew 3–3,' Jeeps recalls.

He was captain for three seasons, with deteriorating results. He led in 13 games, equalling the old record: five were won and there were four draws – a far more common result then than now. His England career ended with the Calcutta Cup match in 1962, but he played international rugby until that August when he toured for the third time with the Lions. His Lions Tests amounted to 13, a record until Willie John McBride surpassed it with 17. They still lead the list, though, and in this era of three-Test tours anybody who tops them will be very good and very old. Think of it: 37 internationals at a time when England did not tour. He was a marvellous player, whose style suited a whole generation of stand-offs.

He attributes his ability to reach important positions to 'simple ambition'. Jeff Butterfield, who played with Jeeps in his first international seasons, puts it down to 'presence'. Butterfield describes him as 'the toughest, hardest player around. He was relentless in pursuing a win. He didn't play rugby for fun.'

All very serious, you might think, plenty of energy needed. But what happened to that excess of energy when the game ended? Well, Jeeps became the joker. He dedicated himself to practical jokes almost as much as he did to winning and achieving.

'Yes, I like a lark,' says Jeeps, now in his 60th year. 'Give me a bucket of water, a firework or a nearby swimming-pool and somebody is going to get a surprise.'

He authenticates two of numerous pranks. 'I got fed up with a long-winded president in Paris and the equally long-winded interpreter, so I crept under the top table and exploded a banger. And in South Africa I took exception to the vice-captain's sweater. He was careless enough to parade past the swimming-pool wearing it. In he went.'

Butterfield believes that 'part of his essential gear contained a catapult: he was just a grown-up Just William'. Sandy Sanders and Ron Jacobs, the props in Jeeps's first international, differ. 'He was a water-pistol man,' says Sanders, while Jacobs has distinct memories of 'raw eggs in your suit pocket'.

It was a time when over-the-top behaviour was not met with a suspension or reprimand and, after all, if the Chairman of the Selectors, Carston Catcheside, could perform a full strip at an after-match banquet in Paris ('the lady violinist skipped out just before the last garment came down,' Jeeps remembers), the players were entitled to be frivolous.

Perhaps Jeeps needed an outrageous sense of fun because a scrum-half took more of a pasting under the old laws.

'But he was India-rubber,' says Rutherford, whose début coincided with Jeeps's ascent to the captaincy. 'He could go through forwards and emerge the other side with the ball. He was totally courageous and a brilliant, inspirational captain.'

'He was a masterly reader of the game, with good judgment and he tackled soundly,' Jacobs remembers.

'He was dedicated, exuberant, analytical and a great team-mate,' says Sanders.

Jeeps played for Cambridge City and Bedford as a schoolboy before moving to Northampton, then one of the top three or four clubs. He clearly might have played for England earlier because he was named for that 1955 South Africa tour, though remained uncapped.

'It must have been one of the Welsh selectors on the Lions panel who influenced the choice because I had a really good game against Cardiff.'

Still, Johnny Williams, England number one, was expected to play in the Tests, but Jeeps and Cliff Morgan, who had booked the Test stand-off place, fitted together promisingly. Morgan, then an old hand of 17 Welsh internationals, says: 'I thought, here's a cheeky fellow. Tons of confidence and best of all he puts the ball in front of me – where I like it.' So they were partners in all the Tests.

'That must still be one of the most exciting series ever,' Jeeps reflects. 'We

DICKIE JEEPS' 'STYLE SUITED A WHOLE GENERATION OF STAND-OFFS'

had two close wins and they beat us comfortably twice. Cliff, scooting over the top of their hard grounds, is still a legend there. We were a privileged group then, *and* when I went back in 1962 and also in New Zealand in 1959. We won only the last Test in New Zealand after two wins in Australia, and back in South Africa in 1962 we went down 3–0 after a draw in the first Test.'

Jeeps was omitted immediately after his first England cap in January 1956, but he began a glorious run from 1957 onwards, when England were Grand Slam winners and then champions a year later. After a dour 1959, with only three penalties from the four games, Jeeps took charge.

'We had captaincy by committee because there were some old campaigners in the pack and we decided that I would break more often and the wings would get a run. Left wing Jim Roberts scored twice in the first half against Wales and we rattled up seven tries and 46 points that year, very high for the game played then, and we shared the Championship.'

Jeeps has fond memories of both Morgan and the glittering Richard Sharp, brought in the day before that Welsh game, but has an even softer spot for Ricky Bartlett, his partner in 1957 and '58.

'He made it easy for the three-quarters by attracting tacklers and timing his passes, and for the forwards by his precision kicking.'

Top of his list of three-quarters are Butterfield, 'the classic centre', and Peter Jackson – 'He didn't have blinding pace, but he made space for himself'. Of his forwards, 'Peter Robbins was a tremendous asset at flanker' and 'the great pair of locks, David Marques and John Currie, gave us so much ball'.

As his playing career wound down he became Eastern Counties' representative on the RFU Committee. 'That was unexpected because Tommy Hall died when due to take up the job.' It is very rare for an active player to be on the committee.

There was one last successful season at Northampton in 1964. 'We decided to get the ball into the three-quarters' hands as early and as often as possible, and both wings, Andy Hancock and Keith Savage, broke the club's try-scoring record. I am proud of that.'

He was an international selector from 1965 to 1972 and when he became President of the Rugby Union in 1976, England had just endured the second of the two 1970s' whitewashes. He was determined to lift the results back to respectability. During the autumn his speeches always referred to the most important date of his Presidency – '15 January, when we start against Scotland. We have to begin winning again.' He took the novel step of writing to each player telling them: 'England expects.' Result: England 26, Scotland 6. Then Ireland were beaten, but England were still nowhere near good enough to take on the 1970s' giants, Wales and France, though that, too, came within three years.

Administratively, he innovated hour-long press conferences after committee meetings. 'Open government,' he called it.

Almost immediately after the Presidency Jeeps, by now a CBE, was asked to become Chairman of the Sports Council by sports minister Denis Howell.

'I refused at first, because I did not approve of what they were doing. Anyway, he came back a week after and I asked him for a job description, which surprised him because they had never been asked for such a thing before.'

He had seven years at the Sports Council and rates the 'Sport For All' initiative and the creation of facilities in the inner cities specifically for the millions of unemployed as his major achievements. He resigned when he had a personality and policy clash with Minister Neil McFarlane.

Since 1985 his contacts with the rugby and sporting world have diminished. A fruit farmer for most of his adult life, he sold the farm and is now a restaurateur at Stocks, which is 'on the road between Cambridge and Newmarket – ideal for pre-race or after-race dinner, whether you've beaten the bookies or not. Mind you, we've got a swimming-pool, so put a change of clothes in the boot,' mine host advises.

RICHARD SHARP
England Outside-Half
1960–67

TERRY O'CONNOR

For a rare breed of footballer, the international stadium becomes the stage upon which they sparkle for fleeting moments, captivating capacity crowds and millions of television viewers. Spectators may be cast down or elevated by the result, but always united in talking about one individual whose magical moments of achievement they will remember long after the score becomes an uncertain memory.

Such a player was Richard Adrian William Sharp OBE. Teak-hard props, salmon-leaping lock forwards and fierce-tackling flankers occasionally linger in the mind. But when a back is gifted with the power to change a game by one breathtaking run to destroy the opposition, he creates a new dimension which never fades.

It also helps if the hero has certain characteristics that appeal to his own supporters. Sharp's extra advantage was his 100 per cent English image, although he was born in India. Six-foot tall, fair-haired, pale complexion, he looked the complete thoroughbred. As an Oxford University freshman aged 21, following two years as a Royal Marines officer, he looked the epitome of everyone's idea of a Battle of Britain pilot as he lined up for his first international against Wales at Twickenham on 16 January 1960. He was almost unknown to most spectators, not to mention his Welsh rivals. His name was not even on the programme as he had been brought in overnight to replace Bev Risman who gained world fame for a series of brilliant performances in New Zealand with the Lions a year previously. An injury during training forced Risman to withdraw and allowed Sharp to enter an arena he was to captivate for many years.

Haydn Morgan, the Welsh flanker known as 'Red Devil' following service with an airborne division, was relieved to discover he was not facing the elusive Risman, with whom he had toured as a Lion. Risman was a

97

RICHARD SHARP BEING CARRIED OFF FROM THE NORTHERN TRANSVAAL MATCH IN 1962
AFTER HIS CHEEKBONE WAS SHATTERED BY A MANNETJIES ROUX CRASH-TACKLE

seasoned campaigner with a Lancashire background and Welsh blood from his illustrious father Gus. Instead, Morgan discovered he was facing what looked like a typical English public-school player. This gave him confidence which was soon dispelled as the game unfolded.

England fielded seven new players, while Wales included seven Lions, encouraging their supporters to contemplate victory. An early Don Rutherford penalty gave England a good start and this was followed by a classic centre break by Mike Weston which created a try for wing Jim Roberts. Wales might have recovered but for a shattering move just before half-time.

The instigator was Sharp, who had already confounded Morgan with his ability to carve deep holes in the Welsh defence. Attacking from the half way line, Sharp again ripped through his opponents with a long incisive run before linking up with Weston. Roberts went over again, with John Young unneeded in support. England led 14–0 at half-time and Wales could reply only with two Terry Davies penalties.

After this match everyone in rugby had heard of Sharp. England followed this by beating Ireland 8–5 and Scotland 21–12 to win the Triple Crown, but a 3–3 draw with France in Paris prevented them from adding the Grand Slam. Even in that final match Sharp made an impact when he glided through the French defence setting up a try for Weston, then worth only three points instead of the present four.

Sharp lost his place next season with Risman returning for the opening game against South Africa, who won 5–0 at Twickenham. Following defeat in Wales, Sharp came back against Ireland and France. Although Sharp lost his place in the final 1961 game against Scotland, during 1962 he was still selected three times by England and as the number-one fly-half for the Lions team which toured South Africa that year. In the early tour games Sharp's uncanny ability to create attacking situations excited the South Africans, but they feared he might cause problems in the Tests. A week before the first match against the Springboks, the Lions met Northern Transvaal, known for an uncompromising approach, especially against touring teams. Lions manager Brian Vaughan was advised to leave out Sharp, but refused to be intimidated. Within five minutes of the start of a game played on a bone-hard ground, Sharp received a quick scrum pass from his partner Dickie Jeeps and swiftly broke the first line of defence. Mannetjies 'little man' Roux, a 5ft 7in centre, sensed the danger and went for Sharp, tackling exceptionally high and driving his head into the Englishman's cheek bone.

Sharp went on for a few yards before collapsing, his face shattered. Instantaneously, everyone present knew Sharp was out of the first Test – and maybe the series. Vaughan was furious as he considered it had been a deliberate attempt to injure the player South Africa feared. Weston, who was playing alongside Sharp, recalls the incident.

'Roux was marking me when he turned inside to attack Sharp. I am certain we would have scored if Sharp had passed after his initial burst as there was a two to one situation. Instead, he attempted one of his famous individual breaks and could not see Roux coming on his blind side. It was hardly a fair tackle, but Richard never showed any bitterness and even went to see Roux when he came out of hospital.'

The fractured cheek bone cost Sharp a place in the first two Tests. If he had played I am certain the Lions would have gone two up in the series. Instead, they were one down when Sharp returned for the third encounter in Cape Town. Then the team had been handicapped by more injuries which had sapped their morale.

The following season (1963) Sharp was named England's captain and his team won the Championship outright for the first time in five years. It was also the year when England beat Wales at Cardiff, which later became a significant landmark as it took 28 years before the feat was repeated.

Apart from the distinction of leading England unbeaten through a season, Sharp is remembered for his performance against Scotland when he scored one of the most memorable tries seen at Twickenham. It is often repeated on television. This has always been remembered as Sharp's match. Early in the second half Scotland were lured into thinking England were planning to attack on the blind side through Peter Jackson. Instead, Sharp broke from 40 yards out and sold three audacious dummies before crossing the line, leaving behind a bemused defence to the delight of the 70,000 crowd.

Weston played in most of Sharp's 14 England games which makes him a good judge: 'He had all the assets needed. Kicked with both feet, had a deceptive turn of pace, and could drop goals from any position. It was remarkable how quickly he gained speed with such long legs. He was a hell of a nice guy who gained everyone's respect, which is why he proved such a fine captain.'

Following the 1963 season Sharp became a master at Sherborne. His decision to help the school's rugby meant he retired from the international scene at the age of 24. Unfortunately, he made a come-back in 1967. England not only selected him against Australia but named him as captain. It was a tragic mistake as he was unable to produce his former standard following such a long absence.

Sharp now lives in St Austell, Cornwall, where he works as a distribution service manager for English China Clay and still follows rugby avidly.

'The modern game is far better organised and it helps to have a World Cup every four years. I cannot understand how they manage so much training. At Oxford I found it comparatively easy to concentrate on rugby every day, but it was impossible after my student days.'

I was privileged to see all Sharp's England and Lions games and regard him as one of the most talented players seen during a span of reporting for more than 40 years. I also remember him as a sporting gentleman.

SPONSORSHIP
The Good Marriage

BRENDAN GALLAGHER

Sports sponsorship can be a hazardous business as Save & Prosper discovered a few years back in the days before they adopted rugby as their chosen vehicle. This London-based financial services group were exploring avenues of possible sporting involvement and decided to buy General Joy, a talented national hunt hurdler. The much-respected David Nicholson was engaged to train the horse, which was soon being ridden with conspicuous success by the Princess Royal.

Everything was going smoothly until the company's main equine promotion of the year, the Save & Prosper Cup at Chepstow, was being televised live. The Princess Royal was unable to attend, so Richard Dunwoody took the ride. During the race, directly in front of the main Save & Prosper hoarding, General Joy dropped dead.

Undeterred, the company bought another horse in the following season. This was Bobby Kelly, but he proved a baulky ride and Save & Prosper withdrew to lick their wounds and examine the unique nature and demands of sports sponsorship.

According to the Central Council of Physical Recreation, sports sponsorship is 'The provision by a commercial company of money and/or resources to sportsmen and sportswomen to enable them to pursue their activities, either as individuals or in clubs and associations.' It is, or should be, a two-way business with both parties benefiting.

Sponsorship is undeniably playing an increasingly important role in the financing of sport in Britain. Indeed, without the £200 million donated by more than 1,000 commercial companies in 1990, many major sporting events would grind to a halt.

Sport receives more than half of the whole sponsorship cake, claiming 55 per cent of all commercial monies. The comparative figures are the Arts (29), Education (4), Charity (3), the Environment (1), and the National Health

101

Service (0.1). Massive media attention is what makes sports sponsorship so attractive, especially the almost saturation television coverage some activities receive. Even in times of economic stringency, it makes sound business sense to sponsor a sport that appears regularly on television. Brand awareness is the target, something which is attainable at a much-reduced cost when compared with direct advertising.

Save & Prosper came into rugby to some extent by chance but to some degree by the persistence of Twickenham's marketing manager, Mike Coley.

'By 1985 we were in the market for a major sports sponsorship to accompany our corporate advertising,' explains Simon Curtis, Save & Prosper's advertising manager. 'We especially wanted something that incorporated live television coverage and initially we had a good look at soccer and cricket. We particularly liked the image and profile associated with cricket but objectively it was already oversubscribed with sponsors.

'Then came the chance element. Julian Tregoning, one of our directors, found himself talking to Tony Hallett, a Rugby Football Union committee man, at a dinner. Tony was in persuasive mood and convinced Julian that Rugby Union was ripe for sponsorship. They agreed to meet with Sandy Sanders, the RFU Treasurer, in the Twickenham car park before the French international a few days later.'

Tregoning and Sanders hit it off, and Coley's follow-up presentation a few months later cemented the deal. Save & Prosper took on a hospitality and advertising package at Twickenham and, more importantly, an initial agreement over three years guaranteeing the company exclusive rights to all of England's home internationals, except those against Wales, which were already spoken for in sponsorship terms. Matches against incoming touring sides were also included in the deal.

Save & Prosper set 1992 as the starting date of their third stint of three years, worth about £1 million to the RFU. They also sponsor the popular Middlesex Sevens, which extends their rugby portfolio into May.

'It soon became apparent that rugby was absolutely right for us,' says Curtis. 'Many of the players, officials and supporters at grass-roots level are what we call ABC1s – that is, aged 35 and over and predominantly members of the upper-middle market, an important target area for us.

'The big England matches at Twickenham offer a large and rapidly increasing press profile and, of course, the all-important live television coverage. At the time of our initial involvement, rugby was definitely under-sponsored so we also gained exposure in that respect.

'We can honestly say that this sponsorship started well and has just got better. You get to know the Rugby Union officials personally and a good working relationship has built up. Negotiations are invariably on an informal basis with each side trusting the other implicitly.'

But a successful sponsorship does not end as soon as the ink has dried on the final contract. The hard work is only just beginning.

'It's absolutely vital that a company be prepared to spend large sums to promote their involvement in a particular sport,' Curtis continues. 'We probably spend an additional 50 per cent, on top of our core figure, on supporting the main sponsorship.'

This additional expenditure takes many forms, including the obvious provision of press information, by way of regular releases and the placing of large advertisements in national newspapers and magazines, while another nice touch has been the provision of courtesy buses from Richmond Station to Twickenham and back on international days.

Save & Prosper's most successful project has been to produce a directory of British international players, prepared for the company by Alex Spink, a freelance rugby writer. This appeared to enthusiastic reviews just as England were working towards their Grand Slam of 1991, and looks a fair candidate to become a compulsory item on bookshelves of rugby fans along with the *Courage League Directory*, *Rothmans Rugby Union Yearbook* and Michael Green's *Art of Coarse Rugby*. For a comparatively modest outlay, the company have derived great goodwill from the book's publication.

The international weekends are the climax of the company's promotional efforts, with a considerable emphasis on the entertainment facilities they receive by virtue of their sponsorship. The itinerary of Simon Curtis over such a weekend is instructive. It begins on Friday night with a Lord's Taverners Dinner at the Hilton. Save & Prosper's involvement will usually be low key, limited to the sponsoring of the table menus. First thing Saturday morning, Curtis is straight off to Twickenham: by 10 a.m. he will have checked that all the banners, logos and advertising boards are in their correct places – 'Actually, the boards have become collectors' items and many get stolen after the match so our name gets spread across the country. We've no complaints.' Simon will then check with Mike Coley at the Rugby Football Union as to the running order of the day's programme, with particular reference to matters of protocol when a member of the royal family is expected as the guest of honour. Then it is up to the company's 17-seater box at the top of the South Stand to check all the VIP guests are well fed and watered and enjoying their complimentary copies of Rugby's *Who's Who*. Satisfied that the party is going with a swing, Curtis will then nip down to the club room, where another 120 guests will be arriving for lunch at noon.

Tickets will be split within the firm on a regional basis, with the regional executives determining the final distribution among valued clients. (Just occasionally headquarters in London will intervene if the same names appear too regularly on the guest list, ensuring everybody gets their turn.) Having briefed the commissionaires as to exactly who is expected, Curtis will circulate as kick-off approaches.

'I switch off completely when the game starts, with all duties temporarily suspended. I enjoy watching rugby immensely and get totally involved in the game.'

SIMON CURTIS – 'RUGBY WAS ABSOLUTELY PERFECT FOR US'

Afterwards the guests are invited back for tea and will normally linger in the club room where a video of the game will be played back. When they depart Curtis changes into his dinner-jacket and dashes back to the Hilton for the post-match banquet . . . where players and officials relax, and a good many friendships begin.

Sponsors can always take their custom elsewhere but the fact that they genuinely enjoy the game and are made welcome by those who play it reinforces the commercial sponsorship. That friendship also exists among the various sponsors operating in rugby.

'People like ourselves, Provincial Insurance and Bowring all get on very well. Most sport sponsors insist on a clause that excludes similar companies during their sponsorship. Perhaps the three of us are not exactly the same markets, but there are more similarities than differences.

'As a rugby enthusiast I was delighted with the success of the Provincial Insurance Cup which made such an impact in its inaugural year. To be honest, anything that raises rugby's public profile benefits us all,' says Curtis.

Having 'discovered' rugby, Save & Prosper have not been inclined to diversify in any great degree. They support the British Army bobsleigh team with £30,000 every season and have also just finished a successful partnership with the Southern Cricket League, which is centred around Portsmouth, Bournemouth and Southampton – towns that are prime marketing areas for a company looking to advise investors.

'Our basic philosophy is to support amateur team sports. Our foray into horse racing was the exception and underlined the problems of sponsoring a single competitor, man or beast.

'Athletes can become ill, lawn tennis players break an arm, and horses can go lame or worse. Strictly from a risk point of view, team sports are the best bet.'

Surveying the sponsorship scene generally, Curtis mentioned one association between business and sport that is almost universally taken as a model.

'I think the benchmark in our business is the Cornhill sponsorship of Test cricket in England. Their deal is a classic example of a comparatively small company having the courage of their convictions and landing one of the prize sponsorships.

'It has all the ingredients, especially the television coverage which is almost continuous for the duration of the game. But they haven't sat back and become complacent. They work hard at improving the service they offer and as a result Cornhill has become synonymous with Test cricket. The public awareness of their company has increased dramatically. Save & Prosper's public awareness factor has increased by 15 per cent since June 1986 – and that is in our target area, ABC1 adults,' says Curtis.

In many ways a good sponsorship deal is like a successful marriage: the right partner does not always come along right away, but you know instantly when that moment has arrived. The courtship may be rapid but the engagement is announced in a blaze of publicity.

As with all good marriages it is essentially a team effort. Sometimes the grass can look greener on the other side of the fence but strains and tensions can be absorbed as long as both sides talk openly to each other. The result can be a longstanding, worthwhile relationship. Rugby Union is well served by its sponsors. Businessmen first and foremost, yes, but that does not lessen their support of the game. As businessmen, also, they know they are getting value for money, a sentiment surely echoed at Rugby Union's headquarters.

ROB ANDREW
England Outside-Half
1985–

CHARLES RANDALL

It has taken a long time for Rob Andrew to be accepted as the greatest outside-half to pull on the England jersey, even though he has won more caps than any other outside-half.

Praise has been grudging throughout his career, as consistency does not rate as a vibrant quality which launches a thousand eulogies, but winning his 44th cap at the age of 28 in the 1991 World Cup final against Australia has edged him closer to Jack Kyle, with his record 46 at outside-half for Ireland.

Andrew heads England's outside-half dynasty by a long way, though the Royal Navy's W. J. A. Davies would have added to his 22 caps save for the First World War, and for skills, Richard Sharp, with blinding pace, and John Horton, of the 1980 Grand Slam team, could arguably be rated alongside him. Sharp made a spectacular entry in 1960, raising England rugby to fresh heights, and Horton's liveliness and audacity served Bill Beaumont's side so well, but both faded. Andrew's formula has been an ability to combine the skills of a back with a voracious appetite for tackling and ball-winning among the forwards. At Cambridge University he earned the 'distinction' of catching scrum-pox as a three-quarter – perhaps a unique occurrence in the Light Blues' history – and during a career with Middlesbrough, Cambridge, Nottingham and Wasps, he has successfully established himself as an outside-half without any real weaknesses. That includes physical durability. He is tougher than his cherubic looks might suggest.

Christopher Robert Andrew was born in Yorkshire on 18 February 1963. The seeds of a sporting career were sown early when, as a boy, he spent many hours hitting or kicking a ball against the barn wall on his father's farm near Scotch Corner. At school he excelled as a games player, linking with Rory

Underwood, his future England team-mate, in a formidable Barnard Castle back-line.

A former housemaster remembers his 'innate self-belief' and the high standards Andrew set himself. His coach at Cambridge remarks on his courage, good temperament and exceptional attitude. England team-mates note his unselfishness, rugby intensity and a single-minded approach to success on the field through good times and bad – his reliable tackling and powerful line-kicking taking care of the bad times, and his tactical intelligence and intuitive skills exploiting the good. Ask any forward. The outside-half who assesses the percentages and keeps his team trundling forward is a valuable asset. In this sense, dullness and greatness are not necessarily contradictions.

Andrew does have pace, while perhaps lacking the instinctive try-scoring ability of Rutherford and Kyle and the elusiveness of a succession of Wales outside-halves from Cliff Morgan to Jonathan Davies. His awareness as a tactical pivot, though, was never better illustrated than in his first University match as a freshman in 1982 when he moved Oxford's full-back Hugo MacNeill, an Irish international, all over the field with his variety of deft kicks.

Andrew's arrival at St John's College coincided with Cambridge's best years against Oxford. He played in three victories at Twickenham in 1982, '83 and '84, the last one by a record margin of 32–6, and while still a Land Economy undergraduate, he caught the England selectors' eye and made his England début against Romania in 1985. Few people among his critics and admirers alike would have realised then that he would push Stuart Barnes, his Oxford rival, into the shadows, restricting this England-Wales dual-qualified player to only eight caps; four of those came as a replacement, and another when Andrew played at full-back in Fiji.

Andrew is utterly dependable with the ball, as is only to be expected of a games player good enough to score a first-class century for Cambridge – 101 not out – against Nottinghamshire at Trent Bridge in 1984. His kicking ability out of the hands is phenomenal. Against Wales at Twickenham he capped his six right-footed penalty goals by landing a snap dropped-goal with his left foot from some 35 yards in the dying minutes of the game. Andrew 21, Wales 18. A fond memory indeed.

Though a points scorer of stature with Wasps, Andrew has not found real consistency kicking goals for England, and Simon Hodgkinson's arrival relieved him of that burden. The high degree of swerve Andrew's boot imparts to the ball is difficult to control in moments of high tension – which is nearly every minute playing for England. He admits that place-kicking was responsible for his most embarrassing game, when he missed nine out of ten kicks at goal for his new club Nottingham against London Welsh in the John Player Cup fourth round at Beeston in 1985. Nottingham should have won – but lost 12–11.

ROB ANDREW – 'TIME HAS BEEN SLOW TO ACKNOWLEDGE HIS QUALITY'

Praise during Andrew's early career was muted, and he experienced a crushing disappointment when Peter Williams of Orrell was selected ahead of him as England's outside-half for the World Cup in Australia and New Zealand in 1987. He rode this blow like a boxer riding a punch, though, and knuckled down to regain his place with scarcely a word of complaint. England flopped in the World Cup, Williams turned to Rugby League, and Andrew, toughened mentally by a winter playing for Carlton in Australia, returned to England prominence where he has remained ever since.

The high point of Andrew's career before the Grand Slam and the 1991 World Cup was his involvement with the Lions' success in Australia in 1989. He made the tour only as a replacement for Ireland's Paul Dean, who twisted his shoulder in the first match, but he won the outside-half place from Scotland's Craig Chalmers for the last two Tests and the two wins that sealed the series 2–1.

At the start of the 1990–91 season a survey among players involved at international level among the four home countries showed that Andrew was regarded as 'the most improved' player. This was surprising for a man with so much international experience, though it could be interpreted as an oblique reference to the return of Richard Hill as his scrum-half partner.

Yes, time has been slow to acknowledge the quality of Andrew the rugby player, but Andrew the man has stood for courtesy and unfailing sportsmanship all along; everyone seems agreed on that. There is not a hint of arrogance about him or meanness of spirit. If these are the bricks of greatness, Rugby Union is well served.

FRENCH VIEW
Too Much Musical Chairs

HENRI BRU

Albert Ferrasse, boss of French rugby these many years, has this stock answer when questioned on his feelings about the English: 'I do not love them, but I have a lot of respect for them.'

It's an old story: remember De Gaulle, and the fact that the south-west of France, strongest of rugby regions, was the scene of much French v English warfare six centuries ago. So there is no reason for things to be different on the rugby field. You can explain the popularity of the Five Nations Championship over the last 80 years or so on this side of the Channel in terms of the pleasurable anticipation of meeting – and sometimes beating – the 'old enemy'. Moreover, when you talk with somebody like Serge Blanco and ask him who are the players he feels most comfortable with, he will say: 'The Irish . . . because they are a bit mad, like us.'

The French conception of English rugby is, I believe, accurate: it is strong, powerful, well organised and serious, but not a great deal of fun. And for a Frenchman, if it is not amusing, it is scarcely worth the candle.

In the '60s, one French international, going to the ground before a France-England game, had a look at the packs' weights and sizes. He clearly concluded that this time England had gone in for even more beef than usual, and revealed his feelings by declaring, through clenched teeth: 'I hope they will be as stupid as they were last time' – when they signally failed (and not for the first time) to make best use of their advantage.

When the sport crossed from England to France, rugby football became simply rugby, since the French have never believed that a kick at goal was as valuable as a try. In 23 games at Twickenham since the Second World War, France have scored 30 tries and nine penalty goals, England 25 tries and 43 penalty goals . . . which suggests that not everybody is playing the same game. All the same, it was in England, and not in France, that rugby was created, and if only for that reason the French will respect the English.

Yet for years, English rugby had the look of a sleeping giant. With all its clubs and players and its magnificent stadium, nobody understood why England were not the dominant force in the British Isles. It appeared that rugby football was considered not only an amateur game, which is fair enough, but also something of a dilettante affair: just a fitting occasion to visit the pub with some jolly good fellows and down a few pints of beer. In Wales or France, on the other hand, an international game was everything and, above all, a matter of national pride. In England, it appeared to be just a way to spend an afternoon . . . never mind if it were boring.

It is fair to say that things have changed at great speed in the last five years. The discreet and old-fashioned charm of the Merit Table gave way to a League much more competitive that the French one. A curiosity this, when you recall that 30 years ago the home Unions asked the French Rugby Union to stop their domestic championship, which they deemed to be riddled with all manner of sins against the true-blue amateur concept of rugby.

Now the sponsors have arrived too: it is always a bit of a surprise when you go to see England v France, and it turns out to be the Save & Prosper International.

English rugby is much more than top-level international conflict. It is always a pleasure for a Frenchman to visit an English school and see the playing fields that surround the classrooms. Here are the grass roots of English rugby, around London and in the west and north particularly. They tell me that schools rugby is no longer what it used to be. The old boys teams are still very much involved in the social side of things but the major strengths lie in the big London clubs and those of the cities of the west.

The in-depth structure of the English game has indeed changed. Teams like Bath, Wasps and Harlequins are powers to be reckoned with: when they travel to play French clubs they display forceful abilities. Typically, the English specialise in big second rows and a dominant back row: a lot of England backs have impressed in Paris too – notably Underwood, Guscott and Carling in recent years. But, for an eternity now, the trademark of English rugby has, for the French, been the forwards . . . and especially the second row. The big men, from Marques and Currie to Dooley and Ackford, all seem to come from the same factory. Some of them crossed the Channel to play in France, Maurice Colclough and Nigel Horton being the latest to do so, with Angoulême and Toulouse respectively.

Everyone involved in rugby in France had a great respect for Bill Beaumont and his Grand Slam team of 1980; here was a XV typical of English rugby at its best. It put forward a strong unit in the line-out, scrum, maul and ruck, the backs tackled well, there was speed on the wing in Carleton and Slemen, and a clever scrum-half called Steve Smith. Dare I say it, but all too often it appeared that the magnificent work of the forwards in English

MIKE TEAGUE IS ANXIOUS TO GET A GRIP ON MARC ANDRIEU

RORY UNDERWOOD MAKES SURE THAT SERGE BLANCO IS NOT GOING FAR

rugby was being betrayed by the scrum-half. In the '60s and '70s, so many players wore the number 9 that nobody had a chance to establish himself at international level.

Unlike the All Blacks, who have always had firm selection principles, England looked as if they were happy to play musical chairs, wasting much talent in the process. That is the main reason for their failure to win more titles since the Second World War. But England's progress was confirmed as they entered the '90s with by far the best team in the Five Nations Championship. Moreover, they achieved the Grand Slam with the same XV throughout, and were consistency itself. That is bad news for the other European teams – how do the tiny Ireland, Wales or Scotland cope in the future with the power of English rugby? But it is good news for rugby as a whole, for England can put themselves forward as serious competition for New Zealand and Australia, and probably South Africa.

England are back at the top in Europe, where they should have been for a good many years. Carling's team have deserved the praise heaped upon them, but Carling himself might have had an even more glorious year if he had been able to lead my choice of the best of the English caps I have seen:

HARE

CARLETON   CARLING   DUCKHAM   UNDERWOOD

ANDREW   STEVE SMITH

BLAKEWAY   WHEELER   COTTON

BEAUMONT   ACKFORD

NEARY   UTTLEY   RIPLEY

England's record against France up to and including the 1991 World Cup
P67 W36 D7 L24

BILL BEAUMONT
England Forward
1975–82

GRAHAM TAIT

It is no more than an hour's drive from Peebles to Murrayfield, but the two places could be half the world apart – it certainly seemed so on the March day in 1980 when Bill Beaumont's England side approached the outskirts of Edinburgh. England had come to complete the Grand Slam: Scotland were determined to prove an insurmountable final hurdle. The tranquil morning stroll in Peebles gave no hint of the electric atmosphere that awaited the players.

'The mood on the coach was hollow and solemn as the lads were deep in their innermost thoughts, but when we began to pass the fans walking to the ground everything changed, there was a buzz and an air of expectancy in the camp,' explained Beaumont, a Lancastrian whose size is commensurate with his huge popularity as a captain of England. 'It's moments like this that you savour for the rest of your life and miss most when you retire. That's why the greatest motivation for any big game is fear, fear of losing because you may never get another chance.

'I shall never forget how the atmosphere on the coach changed in that hour; by the time we drove into Murrayfield the nerves and doubts had all gone. We were there to win. Budge Rogers, who was Chairman of Selectors, and Mike Davis, the coach, had both given their team talks. Mine was short and to the point: "We know why we're here; if everybody does their job we can win." Additional motivation was superfluous, the last couple of miles to the ground had done the trick.'

England's captain had begun his journey to this day of days as a raw product of Ellesmere College, Shropshire, joining the Fylde club with no ambition higher than the hope of being able to wear the maroon and yellow colours at first-team level. Even his position was a matter of considerable debate. His first game for one of the junior Fylde teams was at full-back . . . 'with little success, I should add,' says Beaumont, who has never allowed fame to cloud his natural modesty.

Eventually he progressed to the second team as a second row and 12 months later forced his way into the senior ranks.

'It's strange really how long it takes you to accept that you are a recognised first-team player. I always had to check the team sheet but in the space of a few weeks I suddenly realised I had played against Nigel Horton, Richard Trickey and Mike Leadbetter. Then, and only then, did it sink in.'

Beaumont was too young for the North-West Counties side that defeated the All Blacks at Workington, though in a way that game provided the second rung up the ladder. Three days later Lancashire were due to play Cumberland and Westmorland at Fylde, and since several players were unavailable following their exertions, the selectors looked to Beaumont.

'I didn't really establish myself with the county until the 1972 tour of Rhodesia when I ended up playing alongside Richard Trickey, one of Lancashire's most loyal servants.'

On climbed Beaumont to an England career of 34 caps – 20 earned as captain – and then to a couple of Lions tours, to New Zealand in 1977 and South Africa, as captain, three years later. In 1981 Beaumont watched his great friend Fran Cotton hobble from the Cardiff stadium never to play again. Twelve months later it was his turn to ponder the future as medical advice strongly recommended retirement after one bang on the head too many.

Typically, his last match was something to remember as he led his beloved Lancashire to the County Championship against North Midlands. Though only 29, this great captain had to accept overwhelming medical evidence.

'There is no right time to retire, but having the decision made for you is doubly difficult to accept. No more playing, no more tours and no more coach trips to Murrayfield – all spelled out to you in one simple, stark sentence. There's no substitute for that special buzz.'

Now running the family textile business and still active behind the scenes at Fylde, the popular Beaumont achieved fresh stardom on one of the nation's most popular quiz shows. 'People may break my captaincy records on the field but they've got a long way to go as regards *Question of Sport*.'

It was easy, he said, to identify the most important piece of advice he had ever received. 'It was from coach Mike Davis just before I ran out at Murrayfield for the Grand Slam game. He just took me on one side and said the motivation was over, just forget about the captaincy, go out there and play like a true, grafting second row and we'll win. He was right.

'When you look back those lads didn't need much captaincy, they were the most experienced bunch I've ever played with. But what many people did not know was that for most of the game Roger Uttley and Phil Blakeway were suffering from serious rib injuries and Fran Cotton had concussion. We got away with it for most of the game but towards the end the injuries started to show and Scotland really turned it on. You have to give credit to the Scots, they came right back at us; I remember spending the closing stages asking the referee how long to go. The funny thing is that the one thing most players dread before a major fixture is the time before the game. You're fine once in the changing-rooms but the morning of an international presents an enormous void. Yet that period is the one you miss most after retirement.

'You look back at the way different players pass the time and it can be quite comical. I'm not mentioning any names, but certain people would read a book – without turning over a page – some would visit every single toilet in the hotel, while many would simply sit and stare into space . . . waiting. I know it sounds crazy but you really do miss those occasions.

'But retirement happens to all of us at some stage – you just have to get on with your life and remember the good times. Even now when I go to Murrayfield I still think of that hour on the coach.'

BILL BEAUMONT RISES ABOVE FRIEND AND FRENCH FOE AT TWICKENHAM

THE MODERN TOUR
Wreckers Passé

STEVE BALE

'. . . on the modern tour there is no point in trying to win friends'

Tours are not what they used to be, and if that sounds like the mutterings of an old fogey my answer is: not true. The thing is that, in perfect keeping with rugby's faltering move into modern times, tours have become serious business. For one thing, they are more frequent. In the old days, which may have been more fun but were nowhere near as rewarding (in the sporting sense, of course), if you did not let your hair down when you were away from home and had the precious chance, you may have missed out forever. Nowadays, to take the hectic example of the English international rugby player, you can be globe-trotting each and every summer – 1987 World Cup in Australasia, 1988 tour to Australia, 1989 British Lions tour to Australia, 1990 tour to Argentina, 1991 tour to Australia. There are one or two who have been on every one of these and, as they are no longer the jaunts they once might have been, that represents four solid years of hard graft. In the twilight of genuine amateurism, you still need an understanding employer.

It was not always thus – mostly work and little play – and it is a matter of opinion whether in consequence things are better now than they were. Until fairly recent times, for instance, most Lions tour parties divided into two camps: the 'wreckers' (yes, that's what they were called) and the restrained remainder, some of whom cringed at their colleagues' antics. The idea of the wreckers, who sometimes even included members of the management, boiled down to drinking as much as possible and then getting up to as much mischief as possible in the time-honoured – if that's the word – fashion of rugby-men on tour down the ages. Most of the time it was more or less harmless fun but when it entailed hurling bedsteads from upper-storey hotel windows it was no joke. How they ever managed to win their matches in between the nonsense is a mystery.

There is something of this in every rugby tour, even today, as the list of Welsh clubs which have been banned from hotels in various parts of England testifies, though the modern international rugby tourist is more akin to a cloistered monk than the reprobates of old. No drink, no hanky-panky, a dedication to training and playing the game that might have been claimed by the boys of the older brigade but not with any real justification. Perhaps it was the 1971 Lions tour to New Zealand, when the British players suddenly realised that taking themselves and the game seriously could considerably help in beating the All Blacks, followed by the even more triumphant 1974 tour of South Africa, that made the difference. Today tours, into and out of Britain, are shorter and more to the point. The wreckers – well, most of them – are no more, and rugby's image is the better for it. As the amateur code has professionalised itself, in attitude as well as in actual fact, so it has grown up.

This, I would submit, has been caused at least in part by the eye, baleful or watchful depending on how you feel, of the press. Newspapers first took a meaningful interest in Lions tours in the '50s but for many more years no more than a handful pursued the players round South Africa, New Zealand or Australia. Nor was any off-the-field mud allowed to stick. For better or for worse, there was an unwritten code whereby correspondents concentrated on the rugby and consciously ignored the less appealing aspects of touring – broken doors, beds out of windows, etc. The players played their rugby and then, if so inclined, had their 'fun', secure in the knowledge that their excesses would go unremarked back home. Whether this was right or wrong, it was based on trust and it was not until rugby's burgeoning success, spurred by the success of the '71 and '74 Lions, had heightened its profile beyond recognition that the trust broke down.

It is easy to see why. Even the 1971 team had no more than eight or ten British reporters with them but by the time the 1989 Lions played their first Test in Australia more than 40 British and Irish media personnel – newspaper reporters, television and radio commentators, TV producers, photographers – were accredited. And among their employers were certain worthies who would not hesitate to do their worst if the moment seemed right, which would mean the rest would all have to follow. (One paper panned the Lions when they lost the first Test but a fortnight later, after an anti-Lions press campaign in Australia, faxed the tour management a gung-ho message that its 10 million readers were with the Lions all the way in the decider.)

So, no more beds out of windows, no scandal – or very little. The only unpleasantness of any kind during recent years was when the 1989 Lions' three English policemen, Paul Ackford, Wade Dooley and Dean Richards, asked for a payment into the players' fund from a Perth newspaper for a photograph of them together during the first week of the tour. The paper got hot under the collar, all the British press that were there duly followed up by reporting the incident, and nothing more was heard of the players' fund.

Still, despite the fundamental changes in attitudes and application every tour does have its moments of levity. On England tours these tend to revolve around the decisions of the players' 'court'. This is an institution of dubious repute intended as a morale booster, though I should have thought that sometimes it had the opposite effect. Individuals are hauled before the court for their supposed misdemeanours, which can be anything from dropping the ball during a match to being too handsome or, horror of horrors, being seen talking to the press. When England were in Argentina in 1990 a 'gremlin' was passed on to anyone seen in discussions with a newspaperman, the idea being that whoever ended up with it at the end of the tour would face the wrath of Brian Moore, who had been solemnly appointed judge on the basis that he was a trained solicitor. Somehow the gremlin was lost somewhere between the Andes and Buenos Aires and that particular piece of justice was never dispensed.

Summary verdicts were, however, passed on the final night in Buenos Aires which entailed, as punishment, excessive drinking before the post-second Test dinner and the enforced wearing of unflattering apparel. The hideous vision of the hulking Moseley prop Mark Linnett clad in a grotesque nappy – at least, I think it was a nappy – remains with those who witnessed it. Before the dinner started the England management took fright and rather than offend their hosts, ordered everyone back into best bib and tucker. Will Carling, the England captain, performed a personal miracle in keeping the Harlequin stiff upper lip and completing his speech coherently, despite the enforced pre-prandial consumption of what can best be described as a Mickey Finn.

Players' courts were the brain-child of the English and it is fair to say they would not have been the same without the gravitas of Paul Rendall. The greying Wasps prop is known by the sobriquet 'Judge', for the very reason that this is what he is in his own court. It is a highly vulnerable position because the harsher the justice Rendall dispenses the harsher will be the punishment meted out to him when the roles, by tradition, are reversed and he is put in the dock at the end of the tour.

Some of his decisions have left a lasting impression. England began their 1988 trip to Australia in Mackay, a seaboard town in upstate Queensland which ill prepared them for the rigours of what followed. The first week was spent within earshot of the lapping Pacific in an out-of-town Shangri-la called Ko Huna Village Resort, a series of hutments doubling as hotel rooms designed to make you think you were lotus-eating in the South Seas. The accoutrements were deliberately Polynesian right down to the totem pole next to the swimming pool. An idyll? Not for John Bentley, whose misfortune it was to be the first to fall foul of the court and Judge Rendall. While the rest of the party were tucking in to a poolside barbeque, Bentley was strapped to the pole for the entire evening and made to sing a song every few minutes. Some of the other things that were done to him in in the name of Justice do not bear repetition, but suffice to say that when Bentley, a wing with Sale

PAUL RENDALL ON DUTY . . .

. . . AND ON TOUR (HE HASN'T REALLY EATEN THE ELEPHANT THAT THIS BONE
BELONGED TO AT A NATURE PARK NEAR PORT ELIZABETH) . . .

... AND FRAN COTTON ON DRUMS ... AT A BRIE-BULEE IN VANDERBIJI PARK, NEAR
JOHANNESBURG

who won a couple of caps, returned home, he turned professional almost
immediately with Leeds Rugby League club.

As striking an improvement as any in recent years is the way players are
treated when they go away. These days, long-haul flights are made business
class and the hotels are of the best available standard: in Argentina, England
were ensconced for most of the tour amid the opulence of the Buenos Aires
Sheraton. Past reality was different. In 1988 it hit England after they had
left Mackay. They played South Australia in Adelaide – not a city normally
included on the rugby circuit – and stayed in a motel adjacent to the Australian
formula-one grand prix course which was so forbidding that they dubbed it
the Bates Motel, as it was such a vivid reminder of the setting for Hitchcock's
film *Psycho*. Each room had its own shower, complete with shower curtain,
but somehow I do not think they were put to much use.

This was the last tour of Australia on which some of the press routinely
shared the same hotels, including the Bates Motel, as the players. By 1989,
when the Lions were in Australia (still flying economy), the decision had
been made to keep the two not necessarily complementary groups separate –
which may have been a minor inconvenience for the story-seekers but was
the inevitable consequence of the size of the army of pressmen reporting
the tour. Not all players are suspicious of the press but many are, and

as the game's liberalised idea of amateurism has taken greater hold, so the barriers have grown higher, as the less than comfortable relationship that developed during England's Grand Slam demonstrated. Tours are when the two groups are closest most of the time, and the potential for friction is clear. A tabloid writer told me in 1988 that his paper was not interested in rugby unless there was a row to report, but by the time of the Grand Slam this had been reversed so that the same paper was in constant attendance in the self-fulfilling knowledge that rows were as good as certain.

The Lions' tour of Australia in 1989 was extremely tense and intense, indeed as intense an experience as any of those involved – off the field as well as on – will ever undergo (and that includes World Cups). A three-Test series is bound to engender frayed nerves when you are one down and two to play, as the Lions were, and, although the general relationship was good, the tour did have its bad moments. One that sticks in the mind came after the mid-week match that followed the first-Test defeat. Playing Australian Capital Territory in Canberra, the Lions trailed 18–4 after half an hour, and the tour seemed as good as dead. Astonishingly, they eradicated the deficit within another 17 minutes and the tour lived on when they proceeded to a 41–25 win.

The point of contention was the obsessively muscular, forward-orientated tactic the Lions had used in their fight-back and – more broadly – how seriously they were feeling the strain of Test defeat and an impending mid-week that had turned into a crucial victory. With the post-match press conference barely begun, I remember addressing questions on these subjects to Ian McGeechan, the coach, at which point – with McGeechan about to answer – the manager, Clive Rowlands, stood up, said: 'You make it sound as if we lost by 20 points,' added, 'Right, come on then,' and led a walk-out of McGeechan, co-coach Roger Uttley and captain-for-the-day Donal Lenihan.

Rowlands is a passionate Welshman and this was an unguarded and uncharacteristic reaction to the difficulty of the moment. The next day, when I caught up with McGeechan on our return to Brisbane, he willingly answered precisely the same questions I had asked and intended asking the previous day before Rowlands interjected. McGeechan demonstrated the epitome of tour etiquette: polite, patient, reasonably frank, but without ever threatening his players' confidence, and above all, friendly. The surest way to get the press on your side on tour is to make them feel part of the team, even if you do not really mean it. Here McGeechan succeeded to perfection.

The Lions' great recovery to win the 1989 series 2–1 was accompanied by a virulent Australian press campaign against them. This was the summer of English cricketing humiliation in the Ashes series, and just as the Aussies love crowing about a winner, they cannot bear the thought of a loser. It was an uneasy couple of weeks in which to be a Pom Down Under, both because we were winning and because we were losing, if you see what I mean.

The contrast with the England tour to Argentina a year later could not have been greater, even though the visit was made with some trepidation. When England had last been in Argentina, in 1981, there had been considerable unpleasantness over the Falkland Islands, and this was the first tour by a major British sporting organisation since the war in 1982.

In the event we need not have worried, because the Argentinians were so pleased with the renewed sporting contact – and the improved diplomatic contact they perceived following from it – that the welcome was over-whelming. The England party arrived in Buenos Aires less than 24 hours after the Argentinian footballers had returned in triumph from the World Cup in Italy. In triumph after the opprobrium that accompanied them out of Rome? Yes, sporting history had instantly been rewritten. As far as the citizens of BA were concerned, Argentina had won the World Cup. Posters proclaiming '*Argentina Campeon Italia 1990*' were everywhere; even the normally restrained *Buenos Aires Herald* trumpeted 'Champions arrive!'. Another angle was the cover headline of one sports magazine, 'Much more than champions . . .' The President, Carlos Menem, bizarrely eulogised the team's 'fair play and lack of fouls' when he greeted them on the balcony of Government House.

Thankfully, Argentine rugby is less hysterical. Though also less popular, it is the country's second-biggest winter sport. The atmosphere at rugby Test matches at Veléz Sarsfield stadium is scarcely less intimidating than it is across the city for soccer at the River Plate stadium. But for the real flavour of rugby in its Argentine heartland you needed to go with England – or France or the New Zealand Maoris who had preceded them – to San Miguel de Tucumán, capital city of the Tucumán province which is tiny geographically but is rugby-mad and Argentina's champion province. It could be argued that England's tour went wrong specifically because they were so worried about Tucumán that they neglected to prepare properly for their games in Buenos Aires and elsewhere.

As it happened, they won in Tucumán and, given the lurid stories they had heard in advance about the 'Garden of Argentina', that was a wonderful achievement. In San Miguel the streets are lined with orange trees laden with fruit that Tucumános enjoy throwing at visiting rugby teams. Sometimes it is not just fruit that is thrown: when the Maoris were there bath-taps and bottles were among the detritus recovered from the pitch afterwards. It was in Tucumán in 1988 that the Maoris were engaged in a running battle whose perverse culmination was the dismissal of the All Black prop Steve McDowell. Finally Wayne Shelford, the Maori captain, threatened to take his team off unless the referee did something to protect them.

In Tucumán this can be a problem. The Tucumános have an inbred antipathy to Porteños (people from Buenos Aires, to whom they generally add the imprecation '*Hijo de puta*', son of a bitch), and in 1990 it became so bad that referees from the capital mounted a collective boycott of Tucumán, which is far into the interior. They relented in time for a brave man called José-Luis Rolandi to take the England game. The tourists won narrowly, assisted by Señor Rolandi's penalty awards. 'Rolandi – thief!' bellowed the crowd in unison. This was one of those rugby experiences a correspondent never forgets, a seething atmosphere for a poundingly exciting game played out before an audience who lived every moment as fully as the players. A Union flag was burned on the terraces before kick-off. Was this a Falklands protest? No, we were assured. All who come to Tucumán have their flag burned, so it was nothing personal.

Being in Tucumán is like being in South Wales, the Scottish Borders, Gloucester or Cornwall. Rugby is the sporting king. Because of the locals' passion, England were lauded and lorded in a way that is not familiar either to them, the Lions or any other of the home countries when they are in foreign parts. To make the point, when England were in Australia in 1988 a senior Queensland Rugby Union official who became involved in administering the game worldwide described them as 'the biggest bloody cheats I've ever seen in my life'. And when the Lions were there a year later they were subjected to an irrational vilification such as would never have been countenanced back home. True, the Lions did not take any prisoners, as the jargon has it, but they were at least as innocent as the Australians. What they and their reception showed was that on the modern tour there is no point in trying to win friends. That and the winning of matches have become incompatible.

WILL CARLING
England Centre 1988–

CHRIS JONES

William David Charles Carling embodies the new breed of England rugby player. His position as captain has also made him the figurehead on the march towards a game that now officially allows players to cash in on their rugby game from non-rugby-related activities. It is not Carling's fault that the new rules governing this contentious state of affairs allow huge grey areas of interpretation.

Many of the 'old school', determined to hang on to the amateur ethos of rugby at all costs, identify Carling as a principal target for attack. He drives a large Mercedes and runs his own company, established squarely on his fame and ability to motivate.

Those wishing to point an accusing finger at Carling, who by the age of 25 has done so much to spread the appeal of the game, do not want to listen to any counter arguments, and Carling has accepted this fact of English rugby life. Though he faces claims that he is using the game to promote himself, Carling does not court publicity and cut down television and press interviews during the 1991 Grand Slam season.

Despite these actions the powerful Harlequins centre found that winning on the rugby pitch did not bring an easier life off it. Every event smacking of confrontation during his three years at the helm has been depicted in terms of Carling versus the Establishment. He does not enjoy the massive media attention but has managed to rationalise the heavy demands and, Cardiff excepted, has coped remarkably well.

The wrath of those on the Rugby Union Committee angered by his apparent arrogance was most sharply focused upon Carling after England won at Cardiff for the first time in 28 years. Together with Geoff Cooke, England's team manager, he made a serious error of judgment by refusing, for the first time, to speak to the media. Cooke was subsequently reprimanded by the RFU while Carling and his team decided to sever their relationship with

WILL CARLING HAS THE IRISH IN THREE MINDS AT LANSDOWNE ROAD WHERE ENGLAND
WON 16-3 IN 1989

the Bob Willis Organisation who had been charged with making money for the England squad as a whole. The break from Willis was, as Carling freely admitted at the time, designed to improve the England squad's image and 'concentrate everyone's minds on the task of winning the Championship'. There were rumours that Carling was thinking about quitting the captaincy but this was not true. However, Carling accepted that the growing pressures generated by international rugby, particularly in a World Cup year, meant that his appetite for captaincy might be seriously eroded. If Carling were to ask to be relieved of the captaincy at some stage he might well nevertheless continue to play at the highest level. Playing for England has, after all, been the most important target in his life. He first announced this intention at the age of six.

Carling was born into an army family in Bradford-on-Avon, Wiltshire, and the Services appeared to be the natural career to follow: his brother took that course. Carling was sent to Sedbergh School and then took a psychology course at Durham University on an army scholarship. At Durham he was moved from centre to full-back and this is a position many critics have suggested is well suited to his all-round ability. Carling does not agree.

Cooke, while North Division Chairman of Selectors, had heard glowing reports about a talented young Durham centre and thrust him on to the Divisional rugby scene. He was at once given a place in the England B team

126

against France in 1987 and was to make his full England début against the same country in Paris a year later. His ability to make a genuine outside break was introduced to the England midfield and he warmed to the idea of establishing a southern hemisphere inside/outside centre combination. He would become the inside centre responsible for straightening the line and offering a constant threat. His compact 5ft 11in frame, at nearly 14st, ensured that he would be a considerable physical obstacle, and personal training routines gave him the speed to exploit the gap.

Seven caps into his international career, Carling was given the England captaincy by Cooke with the belief that the centre would be in charge for the 1991 World Cup. It was a brave move by the team manager since Carling, then 22, was also the youngest member of the team. Carling had been forced to resign his commission because the army could not give him the required time off and now the captaincy would take over a major part of his life away from the pitch.

The 1989 season, which ended with defeat in Cardiff and a missed Championship title, was particularly hard for Carling, who played on despite the pain of a shin injury. The cumulative effect of a punishing schedule cost him a place, because of the troublesome shin, on the British Lions tour to Australia – and the player who had looked a Test match certainty was left in Britain. The rest ensured he would start the 1990 Championship fully fit but what appeared to be a Grand Slam season ended with defeat by Scotland at Murrayfield – Scotland taking all the honours while Carling was being required to defend his style of captaincy. It was claimed that he was not in total control of events on the field, with kickable penalties not offered to full-back Simon Hodgkinson.

Carling's reaction was to go out of his way to prove he was in charge. It was rather theatrical but the captain felt this to be the only way of answering his critics. His routine during the disappointing drawn Test series in Argentina which preceded the Grand Slam season was to rush up and grab the ball each time England were awarded a penalty. It was to become a common sight, as the Grand Slam was won by a team totally committed to erasing the memory of Murrayfield.

By the end of the Championship, Carling was being carried from the pitch at Twickenham after England had clinched the Grand Slam by defeating France. The delirious crowd were reluctant to let him join the rest of the team back in the dressing-room.

'By the time I did get back they had taken my boots. I suppose I was lucky to keep everything else on,' he said.

AUSTRALIAN VIEW
Rose Losing its Bloom

PETER FITZSIMONS

English . . . rugby. Let's say it again. English – rugby. Almost there now. One more time. English rugby. There: got it in three.

'English rugby' has been something of a contradiction in terms these last years . . . at least until recently. If it was English it wasn't rugby and if it was rugby it wasn't English. Even allowing for a little exaggeration, surely even England's fiercest supporters will concede that what the flower of England played throughout much of the '80s bore only passing resemblance to what the game was meant to be.

As one who lived and played rugby in France for four years, I often looked with amazement to England where, despite a playing pool (including the extra Bs etc.) in the region of 200,000 to call on, despite having players talented enough to make other countries weep with envy, despite inventing the blessed game in the first place, year after year English rugby teams would trot out on to Twickenham, Parc des Princes, or Concord Oval in Sydney, and play stuff that was nothing short of dreadful.

After playing against England at Concord Oval in 1987, I remember coming off the field incredulous, thinking: 'Is it *possible* that this team is the very best that all England can come up with?' It wasn't that England's play was merely static and predictable: that goes without saying. It was that there was no venom, no passion, not the barest hint of anything even approaching the damn-the-torpedoes-full-speed-ahead attitude which is so essential to really good rugby.

Obviously things have changed. If I remember correctly, that tour was played about the time that manager Geoff Cooke took over, promising to whip the troops into shape in short order. It was greeted with the usual derision. In January of 1988, when Cooke repeated this promise of an English Rugby renaissance just before the Five Nations tournament started, the French sports daily *L'Équipe* chortled memorably at his expense:

DOOLEY TOPS THE LOT IN THIS LINE-OUT DUEL WITH THE ALL BLACKS, 1991 WORLD CUP,
POOL ONE

HESLOP'S WHITE SHIRT CAN BE GLIMPSED ON THE GROUND BEHIND A SCENE OF NOT SO
CORDIALE ENTENTE: TEAGUE RESTRAINS BLANCO (WITH THE BALL), REFEREE BISHOP AND

SELLA (NO. 13) SEEM INTENT ON RESTRAINING DOOLEY, AND CADIEU HOLDS LEONARD IN
A NOT TOO FRIENDLY EMBRACE, 1991 WORLD CUP QUARTER-FINAL

CHAMP LISTENS IN AS BISHOP CAUTIONS SELLA, WHILE ANDREW COLLECTS HIS
SCATTERED WITS, 1991 WORLD CUP QUARTER-FINAL

BISHOP LECTURES THE CAPTAINS AS KEVIN MURPHY REVIVES HESLOP, 1991 WORLD CUP
QUARTER-FINAL

HORAN AND (RIGHT) CAMPESE CHECK UNDERWOOD, 1991 WORLD CUP FINAL

WINTERBOTTOM SWOOPS ON THE LOOSE BALL, 1991 WORLD CUP FINAL

FARR-JONES SPINS THE BALL AWAY FOR THE WALLABIES, 1991 WORLD CUP FINAL

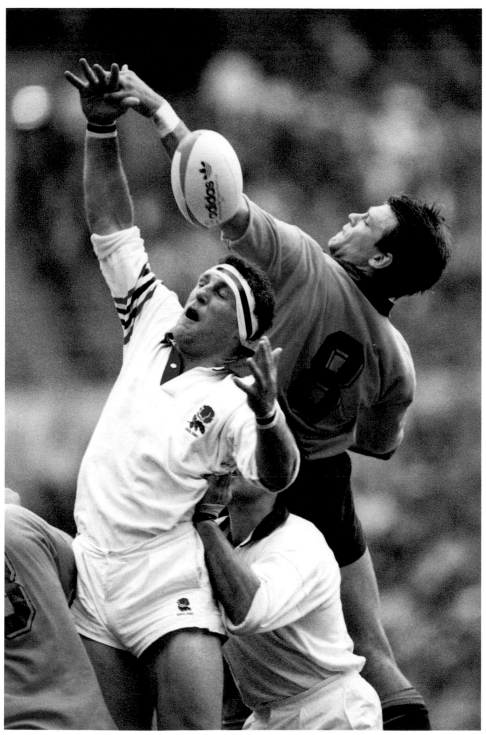

FOR SIX-FOOTERS ONLY – DOOLEY AND COKER (NO 8) REACH FOR IT, 1991 WORLD CUP FINAL

THE MAUL THAT BROUGHT THE DECISIVE TRY – UNDER THERE SOMEWHERE IS DALY
WITH THE BALL, OVER ENGLAND'S LINE, 1991 WORLD CUP FINAL

POIDEVIN AND LYNAGH HAVE PLENTY TO SMILE ABOUT, 1991 WORLD CUP FINAL

'Every year, without fail, out come the trombones from Twickenham, and the trumpeter, spouting forth a new message to the waiting rugby world: "We may not have been going too well in the last few years, but boy, oh boy, this year, *boy* you're really going to see something."'

But, almost as good as their word, England then came within a whisker of beating the strutting and haughty Gauls – at Parc des Princes no less – and went down 10–9 after suffering an unfortunate try in the last minutes. Notice had been served at least, that maybe Cooke's revolution was starting to bite – and the Rose was developing some handy thorns.

As the team's success continued, so too did the respect accorded. Bit by bit the reputation of England has grown. That's the good news ...

The bad news is that, your Grand Slam notwithstanding, we here in Australia do not assess Carling's team as *world* beaters. 'So what if England's won the Five Nations Grand Slam?' seems a common attitude out here. 'Big deal. It's not as if the Five Nations is a really strong competition.' Australian cultural prejudices are such that we regard the rugby of the southern hemisphere as of an infinitely tougher, more virile variety. While the Five Nations is highly regarded as a sporting *spectacle*, we certainly don't put it right up there with a Tyson title-bout or a Wallabies v All Blacks game as a sporting *contest*.

Nevertheless, England are not without their cautious admirers in Australia, including a few in the very top echelon of rugby. One who has watched England's Five Nations performances over the last few years with more than passing interest has been Australian half-back and captain, Nick Farr-Jones.

'There is no doubt that England have improved immeasurably over the last few years,' he admits, 'probably dating from around the time they beat us at Twickenham in 1988; then in '90 they seemed to play particularly enterprising rugby and I really thought they were looking good.'

Then he sounds a respectful note of warning: 'Their next campaign seemed to have a win-at-all-costs attitude and a lot of their enterprise was curtailed, presumably because they thought it was too risky. Sure, they achieved their goal of winning the Grand Slam and I congratulate them on it, but I really don't think that the sort of rugby they played to do it will ever see them through to beat, say, the All Blacks in a World Cup contest. That would call for a return to enterprising rugby, more expansive rugby. I understand from Will Carling that they're planning to do that, which is great.'

Bob Dwyer, the coach of Australia, echoes Farr-Jones's sentiments: 'I think it's fair to say that dating from about 1988, there has been a vast change which has taken place in English rugby. Their pack particularly seems to have developed a lot more sting, and their backs are of undoubted talent – but they are not unleashed in the same way that they've unleashed the forwards and they cry out to be used a bit more as a strike weapon.'

Just what you needed, right . . .? – advice from the colonials on how to go about your business. The thing is, while it has long been an article of faith

WADE DOOLEY IS A PLAYER WITH A SUNNY REPUTATION DOWN UNDER

in Australia that there will never be any greater sporting spectacle on offer for us than the vision of Australians whipping Englishmen in international sport, the waters become muddied when New Zealand is introduced into the equation. For our desire to beat the All Blacks is, believe it or not, fractionally greater than our desire to beat England.

The English players enjoying the sunniest reputations in Australia, the big three Down Under, are Paul Ackford, Wade Dooley and Dean Richards. Bob Dwyer, the ingrate, was even heard to say recently that if he were picking a World XV then he would pick Ackford and Dooley in the second row. Beyond

130

ENGLAND'S EIGHT WHO PLAYED AGAINST AUSTRALIA IN THE THIRD TEST FOR THE
LIONS TO CLINCH THE SERIES IN 1989. BACK ROW, LEFT TO RIGHT: JEREMY GUSCOTT, ROB
ANDREW, DEAN RICHARDS, WADE DOOLEY, PAUL ACKFORD, MIKE TEAGUE. FRONT: BRIAN
MOORE AND (RIGHT) RORY UNDERWOOD

them, Mike Teague is admiringly remembered for his prodigious efforts with
the Lions, if not with England, and Rory Underwood is widely regarded as
among the best of the world's wingers. Gareth Chilcott is still universally
loved and revered.

Rob Andrew, while respected as a very good fly-half, is always thought of
as 'not *that* good'. This is because some years ago the then Australian coach,
Alan Jones, in a burst of hyperbole such as only he can deliver, described
Andrew as 'the greatest sportsman England has produced since W. G. Grace'.
It is to Andrew's misfortune that Jones's words, intended as praise, should
be so widely repeated by those seeking to make Jonesy look ridiculous.

The only other player really to have made an impact on the Australian
consciousness has been the England captain, Will Carling, where there is
much interest in his youth and obvious ability, and finally, while Richard
Hill has not made a big impact on us collectively, he has on me personally.
To see the guy captain England in the 1987 World Cup, disappear to oblivion,
then force his way back and play so well, gives heart to us all.

England's record against Australia up to the end of the 1991 World Cup
P17 W6 L11

RORY UNDERWOOD
England Wing 1984–

CHRIS JONES

If record-breaking is accepted as the criterion for establishing a player's world class, then Rory Underwood is undeniably one of the greats of the game. The Leicester and Royal Air Force wing has, in the second half of a seven-year England career, re-written the try-scoring records and put himself at the top of his country's cap winners.

Underwood, born in Middlesbrough to a Malaysian mother and English father 28 years ago, is the quiet man of English rugby. A non-drinker, non-smoker, he prefers to let his playing exploits warrant headline attention. Throughout his international service, Rory has managed to combine a career as an RAF pilot and England wing. It has not been easy and military demands have meant his withdrawal from three overseas tours. But he is immensely grateful to the RAF for their patience, as Underwood's England career has run its course at a time when the demands on international squad members have almost reached saturation point. He is a regular sight on the A1 which takes him from RAF Wyton to training sessions and matches at Leicester and Twickenham, and the constant juggling between his life as a pilot and what is supposed to be a recreation could well have brought a premature end to an international run that has attracted its fair share of flak.

When he is good, Underwood is very, very good. Cyril Lowe's England record of 18 international tries, which had survived since 1923, was erased by the Leicester wing in 1990 against Ireland. The previous year he ran in five tries against Fiji to repeat the personal triumph of Doug Lambert in 1907. The running total of touch-downs is fast approaching 30 and he is one of the all-time top-five try-scorers in the world.

Many of those magical moments in English rugby required an almost balletic performance from Underwood as he dived for the try-line seemingly unable to ground the ball. In mid-flight he has an uncanny ability to transfer the ball from hand to hand giving him the best chance to ground it before

RORY UNDERWOOD'S WINNING WAYS AT MURRAYFIELD IN 1988

his momentum takes him over the dead-ball line. That kind of skill requires considerable courage. A wing exposes his body to the full force of a tackle as he dives for glory. It is a painful fact of rugby life but Underwood has shown time and time again that he is willing to suffer to score.

His speed and strength are products of training schedules given direction and purpose by the arrival of Tom McNab, the British athletics coach. He is now an integral part of England's preparations each season and McNab acknowledges the latent talent possessed by Underwood. McNab believes that he is the most natural athlete he has ever worked with, and critics have recognised that Underwood's sprinting powers have improved with age – not diminished.

He is not, however, a flawless performer. There have been frequent moments when Underwood has, during international and club matches, appeared to be less than enthralled with proceedings. He has been prone to disastrous mistakes like a lazy floated pass intended for Jon Webb in Cardiff in 1989 that gave the Welsh a try and effectively robbed England of the Championship. He could not bear to watch video repeats of that mistake. His kicking to touch is nothing more than adequate while his ability to catch

133

the towering up-and-under means he prefers to act as support to a full-back yelling 'Mine!'

But while there are defensive weaknesses in his game there is one area he satisfies completely. Underwood uses his lightning pace to magnificent effect when corner-flagging: chasing across from his wing to intercept an opponent trying to reach the try-line on the other wing. Again, it takes guts – and skill – to tackle at high speed and, at the same time, twist the opponent towards touch.

There have been plenty of opportunities to put this skill into effect during his England appearances, the first against Ireland in 1984. His path to international rugby included time spent as a child in Malaysia and then schooling at Barnard Castle in Durham. Fellow pupil Rob Andrew and he have matched each other's rugby rise to the top, culminating in a British Lions Test series triumph in Australia in 1989.

Underwood's first England try came against France in Paris in his second game but it did not signify the start of something special. Six games later he managed a second try and then came the barren run that makes his subsequent scoring spree even more astounding. In his first 23 matches for England the wing enjoyed only four moments of elation as a try-scorer, and has described that period 'as if I was just turning out for England and I just didn't have a massive amount of enthusiasm about the whole set-up'.

That particular set-up underwent a dramatic and radical change after England's poor showing at the 1987 World Cup: into Underwood's life came an England management team led by Geoff Cooke. Cooke wanted to make optimum use of the talents of a back division spearheaded by a wing who, he believed, could be just as effective on the right as the left. The inclusion of Chris Oti in the England line-up meant that Underwood had to switch wings. The shirt number changed but the tries started coming at a remarkable rate.

By the time Underwood, arms raised, acknowledged he had played a major part in securing the 1991 Grand Slam for England, his try count had reached 27 in a record-equalling 43 appearances. Coming off the field against France he could look back with pride on the try that took England to the Triple Crown in Ireland and the score that was so crucial as the French tried to run all the way to the Grand Slam.

SOUTH AFRICAN VIEW
The Television Watchers

A. C. PARKER

The resurgence in England's rugby fortunes was followed with intense interest on television in South Africa, though some scepticism remained as to whether Will Carling's men were capable of wresting the World Cup from the grip of New Zealand. One reason was that five months after lock Gary Whetton's All Blacks outclassed the Tricolors 24–3 and 30–12 on French soil, England edged to the Grand Slam at Twickenham 21–19 against Serge Blanco's exciting but undisciplined side.

However, this scepticism is tempered by a wholesome new respect for the well-drilled, physically powerful and ball-winning efficiency of the England pack, the consummate ability of fly-half Rob Andrew and scrum-half Richard Hill to keep it advancing and, not least, the lethal goal-kicking accuracy of full-back Simon Hodgkinson. Although France outscored England 3–1 in tries, the home side commanded at least 60 per cent of the play territorially. The fact that Hodgkinson kicked a record number of points (60) in the series is a tribute to the effective work of the forwards and Andrew's masterly tactical kicking, which ensures that most of the game is played in the opposition's half, with the consequent concession of kickable penalties under pressure.

Good judges in the Republic were ready to entertain the notion that England, inspired by a supportive crowd of 70,000, might well upset the All Blacks in their first-round Cup-tie. Frankly, until the recent Grand Slam, their World Cup aspirations were not taken seriously in South Africa – this despite the fact that the biggest margin of the Springboks' five victories at Twickenham to date has been 7–0 (in 1932) against a 3–3 draw at Crystal Palace in 1906 and an 8–11 defeat at Twickenham on the demo-ridden tour of 1969. South Africa won two of the three tests in the Republic, but England's 18–9 victory at Ellis Park, Johannesburg, must rank as one of the biggest upsets in the realm of international rugby. The tourists, captained by an outstanding hooker in John Pullin, had come out on a short seven-match

135

JOHN HALL RACES CLEAR TO SCORE IN DURBAN AGAINST CURRIE CUP B SECTION IN 1984
WITH JOHN HORTON IN SUPPORT. ERROL TOBIAS AND (RIGHT) REFEREE STEVE STRYDOM
LOOK ON

HUW DAVIES PICKS UP UNDER CLOSE SURVEILLANCE BY DANIE GERBER DURING THE ELLIS
PARK INTERNATIONAL DEFEAT OF 1984

campaign as 'no hopers' – having finished bottom in the Five Nations with four defeats. Yet on that June day in 1972 England fully deserved to confound the pundits. They led 9–6 at half-time – three penalties kicked by the admirably steady Sam Doble to two by the Springbok fly-half Dawie Snyman. Alan Morley, the Bristol wing, crossed for the only try in the second half and Doble converted it, whilst adding a fourth penalty goal to England's score against a third by Snyman. The England back row of Tony Neary, Andy Ripley and John Watkins, together with a tight five that included Peter Larter, Chris Ralston and Mike Burton, were all heroes, and the halves, Alan Old and Jan Webster, completely outplayed their opposites. It would have been a travesty of justice had the Springboks won through the numerous kickable penalties they were awarded by a South African referee – and missed.

However, honesty compels me to say that this was the weakest Springbok Test display I have seen and reported over a period of 40 years. Tom van Vollenhoven, the former Springbok and St Helens wing, described the South African team's play as 'unbelievably poor', and it was no surprise that seven of them never again wore the green and gold.

Twelve years later England, captained by the Cardiff lock, John Scott, won four of their five provincial games and were unlucky not to beat Currie Cup champions Western Province in a 15-all draw at Newlands. But they were utterly outplayed in both Tests by a Springbok team led by flanker Martiens Stofberg – losing 33–15 in Port Elizabeth and 35–9 in Johannesburg. Only 'Dusty' Hare, fly-half John Horton, and his partner Richard Hill, together with loose forwards Peter Winterbottom and Chris Butcher, were impressive. A youthful Gloucester number 8, Mike Teague, was unable to command a Test place.

Comparatively few England players have excelled in the five post-war Lions tours between 1955 and 1980. Among the notable exceptions were the England centres Jeff Butterfield and Phil Davies, in the 1955 side led by Irish lock Robin Thompson. Butterfield's straight running, elusiveness and beautiful passing complemented the power of Davies, and they are rated the finest midfield pair to have visited South Africa. The tourists thrived on the hard fast pitches. Dickie Jeeps, the then uncapped Northampton scrum-half, was chosen for all four Tests, which were shared at two each. Jeeps again played in all four Tests for the 1962 Lions, and to great effect, but Richard Sharp played in only the last two after being injured, and the tourists lost the last three Tests after drawing the first. English players found Test places hard to obtain. Of the four England forwards in the party, only open-side flanker 'Budge' Rogers succeeded.

Tom Kiernan's 1968 Lions had also to be content with a draw and three Test defeats against Dawie de Villiers' Springboks. Again places for England players were at a premium: only two – Keith Savage (wing) and Rob Taylor (flanker) were chosen for all four Tests, though Pullin played in the last three after missing the first through injury.

MIKE TEAGUE TAKES ON THE SOUTH AFRICAN COUNTRY DISTRICTS DEFENCE ON
ENGLAND'S LAST TOUR OF THE REPUBLIC

The strength of the 1974 Lions led by Willie John McBride can be assessed from the list of outstanding English forwards who could not gain a Test place. Chris Ralston got in at lock for the final Test because the Scot, Gordon Brown, was hurt. Mike Burton at prop, open-side flanker Tony Neary (who went on to gain a record 43 England caps) and number 8 Andy Ripley were less fortunate. Tight head Fran Cotton and blind-side flanker Roger Uttley made the Test pack on which the almost perfect record of McBride's Lions was founded – one draw and 21 wins (729 points against 207). Only W. E. Maclagan's pioneering tourists of 1891 had previously escaped defeat, winning all 19 fixtures including three Tests.

To my mind the Lions were flattered because South African rugby, following a period of striking success from 1970–73, was at a low ebb. Moreover, the selectors panicked and, instead of relying on the team beaten 12–3 in the tryless first Test, used no fewer than 35 players, including playing a number 8 forward at scrum-half!

Bill Beaumont's 1980 Lions presented the rare scenario of a touring team, with clearly the superior Test pack which gained 60 per cent of possession, losing the series 3–1 against Morne du Plessis' Springboks because of the greater enterprise, pace and flair of the South African backs. English representation in the Tests was strong. Beaumont, fresh from his Grand Slam triumph, hooker Peter Wheeler and lock Maurice Colclough, then with Angoulême, played in all four internationals, as did wing John Carleton. Mike Slemen, on the wing, and centres Clive Woodward and Paul Dodge also appeared in Tests.

England's present pack, unlike that of Beaumont's Lions, have made their superiority count every time, and a remarkable feature of the Grand Slam success was the fact that the same 15 players did duty in all four matches – 20 less than the Springboks felt impelled to call upon in 1974. Significantly, Beaumont's 1980 Grand Slam winners numbered only 19, including a replacement. His pack was tremendous – Phil Blakeway, Wheeler, Cotton, himself, Colclough, Uttley, Scott and Neary. The competent halves were John Horton and Steve Smith, and the backs included Hare, Slemen, Carleton and Woodward. Would Beaumont back his squad against the 1991 champions?

I am inclined to the view that Will Carling's present side is, collectively, probably the strongest to have worn the Rose badge for some years. One criticism is that, with a surfeit of prime possession, not enough use is made of a talented three-quarter line.

What is certain, though, is that rugby folk in the Republic would dearly like to see, in particular, these players who have not yet played in South Africa: number 8 Dean Richards, locks Paul Ackford and Wade Dooley, fly-half Rob Andrew, centres Carling and Jeremy Guscott (such an outstanding 1988–89 season) and wing Rory Underwood, scorer of 27 Test tries. But of all the England players I have watched, the following would be my choice of the best composite side:

HODGKINSON
UNDERWOOD, R.   BUTTERFIELD   DAVIES, W. P. C.   SLEMEN
ANDREW   HILL
COTTON   WHEELER   BURTON, M. A.
BEAUMONT (capt.)   COLCLOUGH
UTTLEY   NEARY   RICHARDS

England's record against South Africa
P9 W2 D1 L6

139

DEAN RICHARDS
England Forward 1986–

TERRY COOPER

After an England squad session in January 1987, Micky Weston, Chairman of Selectors, met the press in the team's hotel for a chat about the forthcoming match in Ireland and there was clearly something worrying him. He told us about a ticket row with the squad, but that had, apparently, been swiftly sorted out. The anxiety remained on Weston's face, though, and now came the news that was inducing such stress. 'I'm afraid Dean Richards has torn knee ligaments and will miss our next three matches.'

Weston's worries were instantly shared by those who would rather see England win than lose. England lost those three matches before, with a fit Richards, before the Scots were seen off.

Yet Richards had been due to win only his third cap in the Dublin match. So why such a stunned reaction when a novice was injured? After all, nobody is *expected* to have match-deciding influence at the start of his career, especially a forward. By then, though, everybody knew that Richards was an exception in many different ways. One of them had been scoring two tries on his England début the previous season against Ireland, when he vindicated those who would have chosen him a year earlier. This début had only just been saved from postponement, though, and the pitch was very hard. Richards had been promoted in place of the acknowledged pushover-try expert, Graham Robbins of Coventry, but he showed the expert what it was all about by manipulating the ball over the Irish line twice as his colleagues heaved the green shirts backwards. The hat-trick beckoned, but the Irish pack collapsed a retreating scrum and a penalty try was awarded.

The shambling figure, socks down from the start, shirt outside shorts, sloping shoulders, clutching a ball at the back of the line-out and crunching into a harassed defence, is now regarded by Twickenham regulars with as much affection as their after-match pint. He confirmed his place in the World Cup Down Under, where deflating defeat in the quarter-final precipitated the appointment of a new manager, in Geoff Cooke. He rates his single most important decision the appointment of Will Carling as captain. Not far behind was the choice of Richards as pack-leader when the core of the Grand Slam side came together to defeat Australia at Twickenham in November 1988. There was also an implicit confirmation that he could continue to play in his unorthodox but effective style. Returning from the Lions triumph in Australia the following year, Richards expected to take up the leadership of Leicester but, after one and a half games, a shoulder injury rubbed out the rest of his season. He is a dedicated Tiger, but seldom went to watch the club. He took the chance to work some Saturday afternoons in his uniform labelled PC941, working out of Hinckley Police Station. As a community policeman he works rotating shifts that sometimes mean turning up wherever Leicester are playing with limited or no sleep.

In the 1990 Five Nations Championship England enjoyed a spectacular but flawed – and Richards-less – season. Many thought Richards might have seen England through at Murrayfield in the decider. As Cooke absorbed that defeat, and another in Argentina, he cheered himself up with the thought: 'We'll have Deano back next season.'

First, there was the Leicester leadership to be assumed in September – under changed circumstances. Leicester now had a paid director of coaching – Tony Russ, former coach of Saracens. In a village-type club like Leicester, an outsider might have had an awkward time settling down. 'The degree of support Dean gave me was a most important factor in my first season,' says Russ.

Despite his high profile and readily identifiable figure, Richards insists: 'I am just an ordinary bloke. I see myself as sitting in a corner and getting on with my life. That consists of my wife, Nicky, and my family, my job, rugby, then a bit of squash and some game-shooting.'

If ever there were the reverse of someone believing his own publicity it would be Richards. 'I get embarrassed when people use extravagant descriptions about me or my play. I couldn't do anything without a team all doing their jobs. I honestly wince when I see or hear some of the remarks.'

The fact remains, though, that those who comment on the game, and those who are asked for their opinions by the professional watchers, know that they would not be doing justice to an exceptional talent unless they went beyond routine sporting commendations. For instance, Wayne Shelford, who knows a thing or two about such matters, having once earned the distinction himself, calls Richards the best number 8 in the world. And some of the adjectives that he rejects might wax even more lyrical if he could find the will to sharpen his athleticism: but if he did he would not be Dean Richards: 'Training is a nightmare. I hate it.' Geoff Cooke's opinion is that if Richards 'got himself really fit it is awesome to think what he could achieve.' 'You've got to deplore his state of fitness,' is Russ's comment. But despite having an unusual shape for a number 8, Richards has never been exposed in the

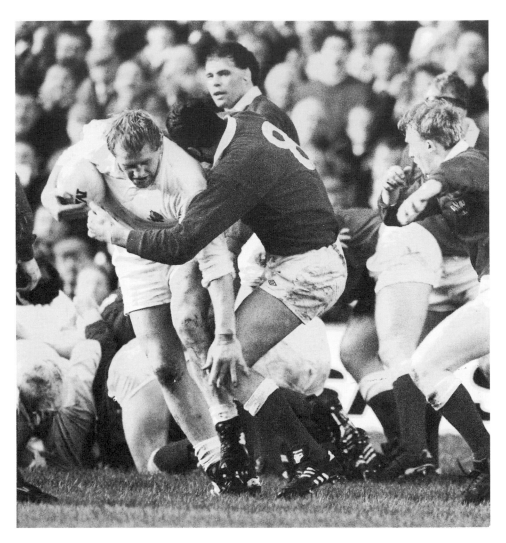

DEAN RICHARDS ON THE DRIVE AGAINST WALES

heart and lungs department and it was he who commanded the scene in the final frantic minutes when England stayed the course for narrow wins over Ireland and France in the Grand Slam spring.

One of Chalkie White's last acts as Leicester coach in 1982 was to choose Richards, then 18, to start his first-class career in the rain at Neath. Since then, Chalkie has followed his Tiger cub closely. 'He is a much deeper man than he gives himself credit for. He has repeatedly asked himself why his instincts have taken him to the ideal spot on the field.' That ideal spot usually involved a defensive catching role backing towards his own full-back. Even his admirers would not suggest that Richards is an exceptional ball-handler in open-field attack. His supremacy is in defence. How many young stand-offs have identified a tempting gap behind Leicester or England's defence and placed a wicked chip behind the midfield backs and away from the wings and full-back? The stand-off follows his kick optimistically, only to see the ball scooped into the cavernous Richards grasp. The stand-off has little choice but to grapple with what must seem like a highly unco-operative polar bear. Then the stand-off's flankers arrive because they were going forward and Richards is isolated.

'But he never goes down,' says White. 'He can withstand the bumping.' Soon Richards' forwards, who needed to turn, get back to help him, the maul is stabilised and possession for Richards' team safely secured. The whole episode has been worked out while Richards is leaning, stiff-armed, on his locks, giving that toothless glare over the top of the scrum at the opposition backs while their scrum-half is preparing to put the ball in.

White agrees that Richards could be a different shape. 'He hovers round 17 stone – he could be 16, a good weight for an international number 8. But he does not try to conceal the fact that he is not one of your streamlined forwards and clearly does not deceive coaches about his attitude to training. And he does not prevaricate when he has a bad game. He owns up to a stinker. Mind you, there are entire seasons when that is not necessary, but he had a couple last season that were below his own standards. Well, he dropped a ball at the start of the Welsh match and messed up a couple of takes at the back of the line-out.'

Richards fans should be warned: make the most of him. There may not be much more. 'The build-up to the Grand Slam and the World Cup was intense. For some, including me, there will be a limit soon,' he warns.

TWICKENHAM, PAST, PRESENT AND FUTURE

DUDLEY WOOD

To have a nickname bestowed upon one can be regarded as evidence of affection, with perhaps a hint of mockery. The Rugby Football Union's ground and headquarters at Twickenham, known popularly to the game's *aficionados* as 'Twickers' or 'HQ', falls into that category. To many it is an old friend whom they like to visit at regular intervals, the mockery or even derision being reserved for the headquarters element or the 'establishment', for it is at Twickenham that the RFU permanent staff reside in an office block in the south-east corner of the ground. The game continues to be under the charge of the RFU Committee, comprising elected representatives who meet for convenience in London, but their proposals and decisions are interpreted and implemented by the Secretary and his full-time staff at Twickenham, hence 'HQ'.

Like all things, the ground at Twickenham is changing and although some may look back with nostalgia on the old-fashioned grandstands and mourn the passing of the terraces for standing spectators which gave Twickenham an atmosphere all of its own, the conversion to a modern stadium with comfortable seating and greatly improved facilities is a development much to be welcomed and is now well under way.

Before 1910, England's international matches were played at a number of grounds including Crystal Palace, Blackheath, the Oval, Richmond, Birkenhead, Manchester and Leicester. In 1907, a fine all-round sportsman and rugby referee, Billy Williams, had the vision and gift of persuasion necessary to induce the RFU to part with £5,572. 12s. 6d. to purchase 10.25 acres of land near Twickenham in order to create a national stadium. Opposition to this scheme was considerable. The ground was said to be low-lying and wet and too far from London. It was to be more than 20 years before the drainage problems were finally resolved and occasional flooding averted. The District Line to nearby Richmond overcame the objections to location and it still carries the bulk of spectators to Twickenham for major matches.

Financing this venture was a major headache for the RFU and a letter dated February 1908 from the President and Treasurer to member counties and clubs opened as follows:

Dear Sir,

You are probably aware that the Union has recently purchased about 10.25 acres of land at Twickenham for the formation of a first-class football ground at a cost including stamps etc., of over £6,000. Towards laying out the ground contracts have now been carried out for fencing, clearing, draining and turfing, amounting to about £1,250. It may be of interest to state that in spite of the late heavy rainfall the ground is in excellent condition, and there are no signs of water accumulation or flooding. The Committee propose to erect two covered stands, each 330 feet long, one to seat about 4,000, and to comprise dressing and bath rooms, office, committee, luncheon rooms and kitchen: the other to accommodate about 4,000 seated or nearly double standing, and to have Press seats, telegraph office etc.

Advertisements were issued offering prizes for the most suitable designs, and it is found that these, with entrance gates, turnstiles, water supply, etc., will cost at least £9,000 more, making a total estimated expenditure of over £16,000. Towards meeting this the Committee have decided to take powers to raise £10,000 by First Mortgage Debentures of £50 each bearing interest of 5%, of this it is proposed to issue £8,000 worth, and the Committee hope that many Counties and Clubs will invest a part of their funds in this issue.

The covered stands, originally designated 'A' and 'B', which later became West and East, actually seated about 3,000 spectators apiece. They were reconstructed and enlarged in the early 1930s, the North Stand having been completed in the previous decade to seat 3,500 spectators. But the choice of the site and the design and selection of construction materials for the stands stood the test of time well and it is a tribute to those in charge of running the game that the Twickenham ground remained for so long in its original form as it gradually built up its reputation as the home or, indeed, as some would say, the Mecca for followers of the game throughout the world.

In the late 1970s it was resolved to convert the South terrace to a covered stand with the upper levels seated but retaining terraces for standing spectators. The new South Stand also saw the introduction of corporate hospitality boxes and a new ten-year debenture scheme with the object of raising funds to finance the building programme. It was opened in 1981 and so the ground had for the first time four covered stands, with a registered capacity of 65,000, of which 47,000 were seated. Hitherto the capacity had been more or less adequate to meet the demand for places, and only for the

DUDLEY WOOD – PLANNING A 75,000 SEATER

England v Wales matches did the influx of visitors from Wales or of Welsh origin result in an oversold position – and cuts in the allocation of tickets to member clubs.

In the last ten years, notwithstanding some decline in the playing of team games including rugby football in many schools, the popularity of the game both as a spectator and participatory sport has soared. It became apparent that some crucial decisions had to be taken about the future of Twickenham. The North, East and West Stands were ageing and, although very safe structures built of concrete and steel, they no longer provided the degree of comfort spectators were entitled to expect. Safety requirements were also becoming ever more stringent and the Hillsborough disaster in April 1989 resulted in a directive from Lord Justice Taylor that national stadia should convert to all-seating over a five-year period. An option which demanded consideration was to dispose of Twickenham's 39 acres for redevelopment and construct a purpose-built stadium elsewhere.

With all its historical rugby connections, though, the thought of abandoning Twickenham as a site and name was scarcely appealing, but there was also another major consideration. Its geographical location, within easy reach of London by road and rail, of Heathrow airport and of three motorways – M3, M4, and M25 – was little short of ideal. Even, it was thought, the local traffic congestion caused by major matches might eventually be overcome

146

by the acquisition of more land for parking and perhaps the construction of a spur road, but that still remains conjecture at this stage. It was therefore concluded that the best option was to retain Twickenham but modernise and rebuild it.

A firm of architects was selected and plans drawn up, initially just for a new North Stand to replace the one constructed some 65 years earlier. Demolition began a couple of weeks after the Middlesex Sevens in May 1989, and piling for the new stand involved sinking more than 300 holes 30 metres deep. The new three-tier 15,500-seater stand was completed on schedule at the end of November 1990 at a cost of £16 million and is believed to be the largest construction of its type in Europe. Designed by Husband & Co. of Sheffield and built by Mowlem Southern Civil Engineering, the main features of the construction are the 21 reinforced concrete columns, each 4 metres deep by 1 metre wide and 30 metres high, with support given to the rest of the roof by welded tubular steel cantilever trusses. At 39 metres, it is the longest cantilever roof in the United Kingdom.

The design work for the rest of the ground was completed by Husbands and approved by the RFU Committee. It involves rebuilding the East and West Stands in due course to produce a horseshoe-shaped three-tier structure facing the South stand, the central section of which will be the new North-facing section. The ground will then have a capacity of 75,000 seats, with an uninterrupted view of play from every position.

Such a construction inevitably creates an enormous amount of unused space under cover which could be used for a wide variety of purposes. A conference centre with syndicate rooms would be an obvious candidate, as would banqueting facilities and a health and fitness complex. At present, in addition to the President's Suite built out from the West Stand in 1986, there are three substantial restaurants in Twickenham – the Rose Room, which takes up to 450 diners, the West Park Restaurant, taking 200, and the Club Room, holding about 100.

Even so, the facilities are not on the scale needed to cater for all those spectators who would like to take lunch on match days and this is the matter which has to be addressed next. Ideally, rugby followers should be able to book a table for themselves and friends without having to pay the exorbitant prices charged by some of the off-site unofficial operators who tend to rely upon their ability to obtain black-market tickets.

But many will still insist that the particular joy of Twickenham is the pre-match picnic al fresco in the car park. On a fine day, to congregate with friends around the boot of a car or estate wagon discussing with keen anticipation prospects for the game is the perfect preparation for an afternoon's entertainment. Indeed, over the years the fare provided has become more and more sophisticated, and gourmet food and wines are frequently on display. The story is told of the Rolls Royce owner who kept his engine running to the annoyance of those parked behind him. When they remonstrated, he switched off his engine and explained, not without embarrassment, that the object was to bring up to temperature the bottles of Burgundy stored beside the engine.

International rugby at Twickenham is part of England's sporting heritage, along with Ascot, Henley, Wembley and Wimbledon. Everyone is keen to be able to say 'I was there' on big match days and applications for tickets from member clubs and schools exceed 200,000 a match. Such enthusiasm and interest must surely accelerate the modernisation and enlargement of the ground. It will not be long before Twickenham ranks with the best sporting complexes in Europe.

FRAN COTTON
England Prop Forward
1971–81

GRAHAM TAIT

For many people the lasting memory of Fran Cotton's playing career would be that famous picture of one of the world's greatest prop forwards in the mudlark between the 1977 Lions and New Zealand Juniors in Wellington. They may also think that particular and much reprinted still frame captured the man. They could not be more wrong.

Not unusually for a big chap, Fran Cotton is a personable, sensitive individual. Nowadays a highly respected and successful businessman, in partnership with long-time friend and colleague Steve Smith, Cotton's first priority has always been his family. On a fateful day in May 1980, in a Stellenbosch hospital on his third and final Lions tour, this stalwart of Lancashire rugby lay contemplating his future, or, indeed, pondering if he even had a future. The victim of a suspected heart attack, his thoughts were with his young family 6,000 miles away. Thankfully, those worst fears were dispelled and a less threatening blood disorder diagnosed. Bill Beaumont, his closest friend and colleague, had sat at the end of the bed offering what moral encouragement he could as the results of the tests on Cotton were awaited. Even when they arrived, the medical answers could not reveal that Cotton's outstanding career was nearing its end. He played only one more international.

'A year later when I watched Fran limp off at Cardiff it was one of the blackest days of my life. With every step he took towards the touch-line I knew he was heading off the playing field for good, but it was for the best,' says Beaumont. Few people realised that the scars of Stellenbosch would take a long time to heal. Lying in that hospital bed, Cotton had to take stock and reaffirm: the family would always come first.

As player, tourist and part-time song leader, this deep-thinking Lancastrian never let his feet leave the ground. He had come from Golborne, a small

mining community just outside Wigan, and come a long way, but now it was time to think about a new life

One thing he would not miss from the old rugby life was the morning of an international or any big match. Even with 31 caps to his credit over a ten-year period, Cotton never solved the problem of how to ease through the tension before trotting out on to the pitch.

'You seldom remember just how the time passes,' he says. 'I liked to lie in bed as long as possible, for the basic reason that it made the morning that much shorter. After breakfast it was a walk but there were times when you couldn't really remember where you had strolled to.

'One day I turned up for a game without my boots and had to borrow Steve Smith's. Yes, he takes a size 11. I got through without any problems but had to spend the next week listening to Smithy moaning about his having to get a new pair as I'd flattened the old ones. He shouldn't have such big feet.'

Cotton is in no doubt about the matches that stand out most clearly in his memory. 'There were four that really stuck in the mind – Workington, Port Elizabeth, Otley and Murrayfield.

'Workington was where North-West Counties took on the sixth All Blacks on a November Wednesday in 1972 at the Ellis Sports Ground.

'The game started at Fylde in August when John Burgess, the coach, explained in clinical detail how we were going to beat the tourists. To put the issue into perspective, no English regional team had beaten the tourists from New Zealand in 67 years and 80 matches. As most northerners know, John Burgess is the master of positive thinking.

'Two weeks before the game I was elected captain and by then everyone was engrossed at the prospect. Few people will ever comprehend just how much tactical thinking went into that game. We played a crash-tackling centre at stand-off for certain defensive ploys, a flanker at the front of the line-out to stop their short-side drive, and any number of varieties on our throw. North-West won 16–14 and that was the turning point of northern rugby.'

Next in Cotton's top four was at Port Elizabeth where, on 13 July 1974 at the Boet Erasmus Stadium on his first Lions trip, he played a fundamental part in Willie John McBride's team that became the first tourists in this century to beat South Africa in a Test series. Even on that occasion, Cotton's mind was 6,000 miles away.

'There was no feeling of elation, no fatigue despite the madhouse scenes in the changing-room. I was there only in body – my mind was with my father. I knew how proud he would be.'

Five years, a number of England caps and a second Lions tour later, Cotton was part of a team that produced a classic display of controlled pressure rugby that beat an All Blacks team by playing All Blacks rugby. 'The atmosphere at Otley was electric with an air of expectancy as the North systematically destroyed the tourists. They were never in the game as the North won by four tries to one. Now that team was a truly great one, but it failed to make much impression on the national selectors. England were well beaten in the international that followed soon after.'

When Cotton took part in England's 1980 Grand Slam culminating in the decider at Murrayfield, he remembers little of the match since he was concussed in the first five minutes. He took that blow, as he did all the rest, with dignity; a year later, he was obliged to close the rugby chapter of his life and, to the surprise of no one who knew him well, embarked on a thriving career in business.

MILESTONES IN ENGLAND RUGBY

JOHN GRIFFITHS

1823 . . . BIG BANG Date calculated by fundamentalists as origin of rugby. William Webb Ellis pre-empted Maradona, handling ball during important game but giving rugby football its distinctive feature. Historians now agree game evolved slowly at Rugby School.

1839 . . . FIRST CLUB Formed by Arthur Pell (later MP for Leicester) at Cambridge University. Matches played on Parker's Piece . . . perilous venue for Oxford forward George Podmore, who had to retire from Varsity match in 1873 when bitten by a dog.

1871 . . . RUGBY FOOTBALL UNION FOUNDED Twenty-one clubs met in London to set it up: 22nd club, Wasps, went to wrong hostelry, enjoyed service and fare and never reached RFU meeting.

1871 . . . FIRST INTERNATIONAL A soccer international between England and Scotland in November 1870 resulted in an England win but caused rancour north of Border, where players held that only Scottish connection with 'their' soccer team was liking for Scotch whisky. Scots asserted rugby was principal version of football played by Scottish clubs. RFU accepted Scots challenge, match arranged for March in Edinburgh: Scots won, but England now lead 52 matches to 39 (17 drawn).

1871 . . . MATCH PREPARATION John Clayton, England international and Liverpool businessman, followed typical diet and training régime of day. Weighing more than 17 stone, trained hard for month before Scottish game: ran four miles every morning in dark before breakfast, with large Newfoundland dog to make pace; four-mile horseback ride to Liverpool office; worked 8 a.m. – 8 p.m.; four-mile ride home to underdone-beef-and-beer dinner. Clayton laid claim to 'frugal and strenuous life otherwise'.

1872 ... FIRST UNIVERSITY MATCH Rugby and Marlborough, pioneers and missionaries, supplied entire Oxford team and 12 of Cambridge XV. Oxford won.

1875 ... FIRST IRISH INTERNATIONAL Irish XV 'immaculately innocent of training' in which several players had never met, beaten by England at Oval.

1879 ... CALCUTTA CUP Polo boom in India diluted rugby interest. Sixty pound winding-up funds of Calcutta RFC donated to RFU, 1877 in form of silver rupees, which melted down to make trophy. First of annual challenge matches for cup in 1879 was drawn.

1881 ... FIRST INTERNATIONAL AGAINST WALES Meeting-point was Princess of Wales public house near Blackheath Common. Welsh must have over indulged, losing by seven goals, six tries and dropped goal to nil. England refused to give Wales a game following season.

1887 ... ROYAL PATRONAGE Prince of Wales, later Edward VII, became patron of RFU.

1888 ... DISPUTE RFU warring with other Home Unions about make-up of International Board to rule on laws etc. Other unions refused to play England until RFU's stance softened in 1890.

1892 ... PERFECT TRIPLE CROWN England – uniquely – won Triple Crown without conceding a point.

1895 ... SPLIT Northern clubs broke away as RFU tightened amateur rules. Northern Union formed, now Rugby League. Cost to England severe, as forward play fell into decline, and no Championship won till 1910.

1906 ... ENTENTE CORDIALE France overwhelmed in first match with England.

1910 ... TWICKENHAM New team, playing at new permanent home (tactics by Adrian Stoop), made England champions after 18 barren years.

1913–24 ... GOLDEN ERA England landed Grand Slam five times, Triple Crown five times and lost only twice – both times to Wales. Cyril Lowe set 18-try record. Wavell Wakefield emerged as father of modern forward play.

1928 ... PERFECT SEASON Only season in which England achieved Grand Slam *and* beat Dominion side (NSW).

1930 ... LIONS CAPTAIN Doug Prentice of England captained British Lions to Australasia – Bill Beaumont only Englishman to do so since (in 1980).

1936 ... ALL BLACKS FALL TO RUSSIAN Young Oxford wing Prince Obolensky scored two spectacular tries as England beat New Zealand for first time, at Twickenham. Obolensky was killed on RAF service early in 1940.

GEOFF COOKE, ENGLAND'S FIRST COACH, WITH JEAN-PIERRE VILLEPRIEUX OF FRANCE AT
A COACHING SESSION IN PORTUGAL

1957... ERIC'S YEAR Eric Evans, who said role of coach was 'means of transport for getting the team to the ground', led England to Grand Slam. Queen and Prince Philip attended decisive match.

1963 ... DOWN UNDER First full tour abroad, including Tests in New Zealand and Australia, where England lost on pitch more suitable for water polo.

1965 ... HANCOCK'S HALF MINUTE England flair for last gasp Calcutta Cup tries extended by Andy Hancock with long solo run in last 30 seconds at Twickenham. Result 3–3.

1971 ... RFU CENTENARY

1972 ... WHITEWASH For first time England lost all four matches in Five Nations Championship. Wales threatened to drop fixture.

1972–3 ... UNDAUNTED ON TOUR Victims turned conquerors with shock wins in South Africa ('72) and New Zealand ('73).

1980 ... GRAND SLAM Bill Beaumont led England to first four-timer for

154

23 years. Key to success explosive match against 14 Welshmen registering 7 on Richter scale.

1984 ... *ADIEU* DUSTY William Henry 'Dusty' Hare retired from international rugby as England's most prolific scorer of points.

1991 ... SILENCE IS GOLDEN Manager Geoff Cooke, captain Will Carling and England squad sent media to Coventry. Welsh supporters grateful for reticence after England's biggest ever win in Wales and their first in Cardiff for 28 years, first step to Grand Slam number 9 by England. Others – Wales 8 Grand Slams, France 4, Scotland 3, Ireland 1. Additionally, Carling became England's most successful captain, Rory Underwood set try-scoring record and Simon Hodgkinson kicked unprecedented 60 points.

AUTUMN 1991 ... £20-A-DAY England's squad took five weeks off work to reach World Cup Final; radically increased public awareness of rugby union; obliged League soccer clubs to bring forward kick-off times to avoid ITV coverage from Twickenham; helped competition gross £40 million – all for £20 per day.

ANDY RIPLEY
England Forward 1972–76

BRENDAN GALLAGHER

Pierre Danos suggested that rugby players come in two varieties: piano-shifters and piano-players. It is typical of Andy Ripley that he cannot be confined to either category. Here is a player ready to move mountains for his team, let alone pianos; here also is an ivory-tickler with a marked liking for eccentric off-beat numbers. The gangling 6ft. 5in. Ripley has never conformed to stereotypes, abhors the humdrum and refuses to nest in any social pigeon-hole. His CV still reads like an over ambitious application form intended to wow university authorities and gain an important scholarship. Ripley has never needed to embellish the truth, though, for he has led a career of conspicuous achievement.

England number 8, author, church warden, triathlete, British *Superstars* champion, city banker, 400m hurdler, motorcycle enthusiast, British Canoe Union instructor, lecturer at the Sorbonne and the youngest ever President of Rosslyn Park: the list has footnotes . . . he loves jazz, real ale and fine wines. Definitely a man of many parts, most of them still working, Ripley took up body-breaking, widow-making triathlons on his 40th birthday and has maintained his endearing eccentricity as he approaches middle-age. He attended Rosslyn Park's annual dinner recently dressed in jeans and a T-shirt. 'I ate before I came' was the message blazoned across his chest. Ripley likes T-shirts. Touring South Africa in 1974 with the British Lions, he went through his full repertoire including his favourite 'I'm so perfect it scares me'.

For Ripley, rugby has always been an amusing diversion, never to be confused with the real world of mortgages, unemployment and political strife. He played with the studied nonchalance of a Harlem Globetrotter warming up. With his flowing locks, stylish headband and spring-heeled athleticism he looked more like a basketball 'dude' than a rugby 'jock'. But was Ripley, to borrow Colin Meads' perceptive remark about some English rugby players, all sweatband and no sweat?

His spectacular injections of pace left the crowd roaring and defenders treading water. Ripley in full flight, knees pumping, hair streaming and the ball tucked greedily under his arm, was one of the definitive rugby sights of the '70s. His line-out capability was undoubted, but his critics pointed to a frustrating looseness around the fringes and his less than reliable handling. A crash course at Ray Prosser's Finishing School for Streetwise Forwards at Pontypool might well have injected steel and cussedness into his game but the essential Ripley would have been lost. And those doubting his grafting qualities should be reminded of his immense contributions at Ellis Park, Johannesburg, in 1972 and Eden Park, Auckland, the following year when England recorded shock Test victories over South Africa and New Zealand respectively. England's win over the Springboks was achieved through forward domination, with Ripley jumping superbly to rule the back of the line-out. His back-row combination with Tony Neary and John Watkins proved effective against the formidable hard-ground line-up of Jan Ellis, Piet Greyling and Alan Bates, and the English trio also performed heroically against New Zealand when the tourists won 16–10, their only win of the tour.

In all, Ripley won 24 England caps, his first coming against Wales in 1972 and his last against Scotland in 1976. He toured South Africa with the unbeaten Lions in 1974, scoring five tries in nine appearances, though the incomparable Mervyn Davies prevented him from winning a Test place, and reached two John Player Cup finals with Rosslyn Park, against Bedford in 1975 and Gosforth in 1976 – both lost.

In Sevens, Ripley's manic running always galvanised any tournament, especially the Middlesex Sevens, at which he led Rosslyn Park to victory in 1976. Sevens saw Ripley at his happiest, with the carnival atmosphere on such occasions mimicking his approach and his exceptional pace making life a misery for opponents. Tom McNab, England's conditioning guru, would have exulted at the prospect of working with such an outstanding athlete.

Browsing through a second-hand bookshop in Galway I was astonished to find, nestling comfortably alongside the works of Rousseau and Russell in the philosophy section, a rogue copy of *Ripley's Rugby Rubbish*. On reflection, the Irish might have a point. Ripley's Pythonesque romp through the game he loves is a pretty fair reflection of his philosophy – his donation of all the profits from the book to charity also spells out a pertinent message about the man. But just as most comedians harbour a secret wish to play Macbeth, I suspect that under Ripley's baseball cap and gauche exterior lurks the desire to write a 'serious book'. That, however, would involve Ripley taking himself seriously, an unlikely scenario. Just occasionally though, you do get the sense that he sometimes has to work hard at appearing constantly laid-back and non-conformist. He counters these pressures by retiring to his ultra conventional commuter-belt house in Dormansland, where he relaxes with Austrian-born wife Elizabeth and their three children. A notable supporter

EASY RIDER R–PL– –

of local charities and a pillar of the village community, Ripley has carved an agreeable niche in leafy Surrey.

Ripley's hugely successful appearances in the BBC *Superstars* championships made him one of rugby's earliest media personalities. His public profile easily matched that of the game's legends, such as Barry John and Gareth Edwards. Every demand was handled with good humour and as Rugby Union annexes an increasingly larger slice of media attention and public awareness, his approach could serve as a blueprint for others.

THE GREAT UN-CAPPED
Chariots Hijacked

BARRIE FAIRALL

Ask a prop who now spends more time in the scrum at the bar than out on the field to write about the finest player he ever saw who never played for England and you might expect him to wax lyrical on a front-row forward. With apologies to Phil Keith-Roach and other stalwart members of the Union, this prop's choice falls upon someone rather more sprightly than those destined to burrow for the ball in an activity often passed off as a game within a game.

After all, as pack members and even goal-kickers would admit, rugby is about scoring tries. In the early '70s, Keith-Roach and his Rosslyn Park colleagues would frequently scrummage London Welsh off the Old Deer Park only to look up from their labours to witness a speed merchant such as Gerald Davies crossing their line some 60 yards behind them. As galling as that must have been, the Welsh in those days had to be admired. One Park member even rather foolishly struck a bet with John Dawes that he would not cut his hair until his club had seen the Welsh off. Two years later and this gentleman – a journalist, no less, and by now looking as if he was about to audition for a rock band of the times – finally had to admit defeat, just as Park had done for what seemed the umpteenth occasion. But for Park, the good times were one day ready to roll with the emergence of a wing the likes of which could have made a stunning contribution to the England cause against all and sundry.

In 1986 Park, seeking to put one over their London rivals in the now extinct and quaintly named Merit Table, were leading by a couple of points with just a few minutes remaining when Martin Offiah fielded the ball inside his own 25. With everyone, including the Park coach, yelling for him to hoof into touch, Offiah set off across the pitch. Fast approaching the opposite touch-line, he then turned right, hit the accelerator and proceeded the remaining length of the field for an astonishing try that later earned him a ticking-off.

OFFIAH THE LION – BUT IN RUGBY LEAGUE LIVERY

The book on safety-first rugby, apparently feverishly read by so many English coaches and selectors, was simply thrown out of the window. On that afternoon there was at least one prop who wanted to see a lot more of young Offiah, and his wishes were granted when the Barbarians selected him for their 1987 Easter tour of Wales. And it was Offiah, with four tries in two matches, who led the parade, besides instigating some lively debate on Park's hot property.

First stop, Arms Park, where a hat-trick of tries by Gerald Cordle helped Cardiff to a 33–24 win. The Barbarians, though, had been 15 points up within the opening 20 minutes. Will Carling had started their charge almost from the kick-off and it was Offiah, haring away down the left, who scored their second try. The holiday weekend was just beginning to warm up because by the time Offiah and the Baa-Baas reached Swansea they were really into their stride.

What the crowd at St Helens was treated to came by way of three dashing tries from Offiah in a 30–17 Barbarian victory. Having penetrated the Swansea defence as early as the third minute, he went clear away again before the interval and completed a wonderful afternoon's work by rounding off another move during the second half. Meanwhile the press

160

box had been treated to a contest of the verbal kind between two former Welsh internationals who now express themselves in print. Clem Thomas, for example, reckoned that Offiah would never play for England on the grounds that he showed defensive shortcomings. Barry John, on the other hand, said that if Offiah were a Welshman he would walk into his country's side. And so the argument went on, punctuated by Offiah's scoring feats on an unforgettable afternoon. If the opinion of a prop counts for anything, then he always felt that England should have taken Offiah smartly under their wing and flown him off to Australia with their squad for the first World Cup that summer.

Offiah, meanwhile, saw out the season in traditional, though as it turned out, painful fashion, by taking part in the Middlesex Sevens at Twickenham. The sign-off was odd in some respects because Offiah was listed to play for the Rosslyn Park 'second' string, one led by that splendid club-man Rad Montgomery and featuring Andy Ripley, John Graves, Mark Jermyn, Nick Anderson and Chris Mantel. Park duly won through to a final showdown with Harlequins, everyone looking forward to the confrontation between Offiah and Andy Harriman. Sadly, both were injured in the early stages and were off the field by the time Quins registered a record tenth triumph in the event.

From sign-off to sign-on: news began to filter through that Park officials were resigned to the fact that Offiah would be switching from Union to League. By July, Widnes had come up with an offer of around £65,000 and, while Offiah held out for a few thousand more, the writing was on the wall. While word of his signing received scarcely a mention in the national newspapers, not since Tom van Vollenhoven, the South African wing who scored a hat-trick of tries against the Lions in 1955, was taken on by St Helens' had a convert to League made such a big impact during his first season in the professional game.

The loss to Union can be gauged now only by the immediate impression made in his new career. In his opening season, the 21-year-old recruit was to top the League try-scoring list with a total of 44 touch-downs, and his finishing powers had much to do with Widnes walking off with the League Championship and the Premiership trophy. He scored a further 19 tries after being selected for the Great Britain tour party Down Under. Widnes, it seems, could hardly believe their good fortune because apparently no one from the club had actually seen Offiah playing in the flesh before he signed on the dotted line.

Offiah did not take up rugby until he became a boarder at Woolverstone Hall school in Suffolk at the age of 11. 'I was very upset,' he says, 'because I was soccer mad and a keen Arsenal supporter. But after I got there and began playing rugby I started enjoying it and I found I wasn't too bad. I used to play fly-half or in the centre, and in fact I was in the centre when I played for London Schoolboys and at senior level for Eastern Counties.

161

'In my early days at school I wasn't exceptionally quick. When I was 13 I couldn't even get into a relay team unless someone got injured. It was my elder brother who was the outstanding athlete and sportsman. When people heard the name Offiah, they thought it was him not me. He was the star at school and went on to play for Surrey before deciding to pack it in.'

When he left school, Martin Offiah moved back to London. He considered joining either Wasps or Harlequins, but in the end opted for Park. By Christmas, he had already played himself into the first team. His Union career then continued with appearances for England Students, London Division, the aforementioned Baa-Baas and the Penguins, for whom he was to star in the Hong Kong Sevens. He might even have finished up at Bath after he had received an offer to study physical education at the university there. But then he had a telephone call.

'One evening, just after the season had finished, I got a call from one of the scouts at Widnes asking me if I was interested in Rugby League. I think they had heard about me when I had been up to play at Liverpool St Helens and seen me on television playing for the Barbarians and in the Middlesex Sevens.

'I got a bit mixed up and thought it was Wigan he was talking about and I remember putting the phone down and thinking "Widnes, who are they?" Anyway, the scout had asked if the coach Doug Laughton could have a word with me and I said yes. I'd seen the Challenge Cup final as well as a few other League games on television, but I wouldn't say at the time I was keen on it.'

A meeting with Laughton in London changed everything. 'I think he caught me at just the right time,' Offiah says. 'I'd just finished college in London and was planning to go to Bath. I had nothing really to keep me in London and I felt it would be a great new challenge, a make-or-break thing which could change my life. The offer was exceptionally good, so I decided to do it. In many ways, it was such a big gamble.'

And so Offiah became the one that got away . . . Union's loss and a huge League gain . . . and England rugby so much the poorer. Even a prop mourned his parting, while England's supporters, with their renderings of 'Swing Low, Sweet Chariot', would surely have taken to Chariots Offiah.

12–6 AND ALL THAT

TED BARRETT

The wisest words on the subject of England's seemingly disastrous tour of Australia and Fiji, which ended just nine weeks before the World Cup began, came from a distant observer. A. C. Parker noted from the 40–15 thrashing Australia gave England at the end of the summer that the 'ageing English pack in Southern Hemisphere conditions is not nearly so effective as in the heavier, softer going at home . . . I still feel, though, that England will fully extend the All Blacks when they clash at Twickenham in October. Home conditions and a home crowd should make a difference, though the All Blacks obviously will start firm favourites . . .' Not a bad assessment.

Expressed as 'Played 7, won 3, lost 4, scoring 151 points and conceding 162', the tour does not sound a complete fiasco, though senior England players had long held that it was the right tour at the wrong time. A triumphant progress through Australia and Fiji by a side unavoidably short of match fitness was not to be expected, but crucially, England lost the three most significant matches in World Cup terms – 21–19 against New South Wales (led by Nick Farr-Jones) in the opening match; 20–14 against Queensland in the third; and 40–15 against Australia in the seventh – besides falling 27–13 to Fiji B in Lautoka after leading 13–3 at half-time.

They returned home to prolonged inquests, official and otherwise. Thirty-six days after the Sydney débecle, the 26-strong squad for the World Cup was announced – showing that the England management were of a like mind with A. C. Parker, and that they had no intention of deserting the principles of long-term team-building. John Hall was omitted because of his chronic knee problem following the full Fiji XV match, but otherwise only three of the summer tour party were left out – Ian Hunter, Damian Hopley and Martin Bayfield, seen by many as the natural successor to Wade Dooley once the World Cup was over. The selection also showed that the criticisms voiced in previous chapters by writers and players from other Test-playing nations about a tendency for wholesale and whimsical changes were no longer valid.

The World Cup teams chosen by Geoff Cooke and his associates were to be variations on a persisting theme, bringing closer perhaps the establishment of a unitary style and purpose in English rugby. The 26 were:

BACKS
S. D. HODGKINSON (*Nottingham*) J. M. WEBB (*Bath*)
R. UNDERWOOD (*Leicester and RAF*) N. J. HESLOP (*Orrell*) C. J. OTI (*Wasps*)
W. D. C. CARLING (*Harlequins, capt.*)
J. C. GUSCOTT (*Bath*) S. J. HALLIDAY (*Harlequins*)
C. R. ANDREW (*Wasps*) D. PEARS (*Harlequins*) R. J. HILL (*Bath*)
C. D. MORRIS (*Orrell*)

FORWARDS
J. LEONARD (*Harlequins*) P. A. G. RENDALL (*Askeans*) J. K. PROBYN (*Askeans*)
G. S. PEARCE (*Northampton*)
B. C. MOORE (*Harlequins*) C. J. OLVER (*Northampton*)
P. J. ACKFORD (*Harlequins*)
W. A. DOOLEY (*Preston Grasshoppers*) N. C. REDMAN (*Bath*)
M. C. TEAGUE (*Gloucester*) M. G. SKINNER (*Harlequins*)
P. J. WINTERBOTTOM (*Harlequins*) G. W. REES (*Notthingham*)
D. RICHARDS (*Leicester*)

Mr Cooke's appointed assistants were to be coach Roger Uttley (Wasps) and medical officer, Dr Ben Gilfeather, with Kevin Murphy (Sale), the physiotherapist. And following the warm-up matches against the Soviet Union (53–0), Gloucester (34–4) and the England Students (35–0), nothing remained by 3 October but for England to deploy Webb at full-back, (Hodgkinson had sprained an ankle) Underwood, Carling, Guscott and Oti at three-quarter, and Andrew and Hill at half-back, behind the celebrated Grand Slam pack. It was to be the last time these eight men were ever to start a match together for England.

NEW ZEALAND'S 18–12 OVERTURE JOHN MASON

It was business as usual for the World Champions New Zealand who wore England down under gun-metal grey skies at Twickenham in the opening match of the 1991 World Cup – Thursday, 3 October. Not, perhaps, the ideal start to a World Cup seeking universal appeal, but the job, for all that, was expertly done.

By denying England possession for long periods, besides snatching important line-outs against the throw-in, New Zealand steadily built the foundations of victory by a goal and four penalty goals to three penalty goals and a dropped-goal.

The win guaranteed New Zealand safe passage, begging the pardon of Italy and the United States, who made up the remainder of Pool One, to a quarter-final place in Lille on 20 October.

WEBB ASSESSES THE HAKA HIGH-JUMP FINALE AS DEMONSTRATED BY LOE AND (RIGHT)
GARY WHETTON AT HQ

CARLING KICKS FOR TOUCH AGAINST THE ALL BLACKS

For England, defeat hurt. The prospect of an immediate exit in the knock-out section of the competition would inevitably dog them in everything they did over the following fortnight. At best, defeat meant that England would need to beat France in Paris to reach the semi-final, which would at least concentrate minds wonderfully. Defeat at Twickenham under the leadership of Will Carling was also an unwelcome experience. As captain, Carling had not lost there previously and the team had been successful in all matches at HQ since falling to Wales in February 1988.

Michael Jones, the All Blacks flanker, the man who says never on Sundays because of his religious beliefs, had no peer though I imagine he will be seeking forgiveness for his one error. As Webb, England's rock at full-back, cleared from the kick-off, Jones arrived at speed. Webb's kick screwed away to the left round about the time the flanker stuck out an arm, Webb hurtled to the ground, Jones apologised and New Zealand were penalised at the point the ball landed. Webb was swiftly back on his feet and successfully kicking for goal, putting England three points up within seconds of the start. The predominantly England-orientated crowd enjoyed that. The chariot was hardly swinging, though. Within five minutes Fox levelled the score after England had been penalised for collapsing a scrum, and five minutes later he made it 6–3 after England had come piling over the top in an effort to win the ball back on the ground.

Webb pulled England back to 6–6 after Gary Whetton had been penalised for a high tackle on Oti – who had cut back towards the forwards and would have gone no further anyway. Whetton was not best pleased. A Winterbottom right-hander allowed Fox to kick his third penalty goal and when the All Blacks pulled a scrum

166

ENGLAND FORWARDS ACKFORD, WINTERBOTTOM AND TEAGUE WATCH HILL GET THE
BALL BACK

down adjacent to their posts, Webb's third goal brought another chariot verse, a shade off key, like, I fear, England. Even a dropped-goal by Andrew following a free-kick awarded for a crooked scrum feed on the stroke of half-time did less to lift England than it should have done. Nerves were still uppermost. By then Kirwan had had a couple of runs on the right, plus a hefty surge in off his wing to test the midfield, but here England did well. Innes and McCahill were cut down time after time and Webb did not let Wright escape when he came up outside Kirwan.

But 12 minutes into the second half New Zealand settled the match. The preliminaries involved a line-out and scrum; Fox and McCahill found some space and, though Jones was held this time, another scrum followed. Bachop scampered right, linking with Innes, who flipped the ball up, sensing rather than seeing his colleague. Weeks of preparation took Bachop instinctively on to the ball, fractionally before it went to earth – a try was on. Kirwan made the breach on the right-hand touch and, when the covering tackle came, the faithful Jones was there for the return pass and a try which Fox converted.

Fox's fourth penalty goal seven minutes later, after Carling had scrambled desperately for the ball on the ground, left England with a mountain to climb. Sensing this, the crowd turned their attention to referee Jim Fleming. The rough ride was unkind: it was the laws that infuriated, not the person applying them – correctly. But there were still 20 minutes left and, with the All Blacks establishing a pace of their choosing, England could find no way to free their backs. Frustrations multiplied and the threat from Guscott, the player the All Blacks feared, never materialised.

Underwood is England's record try-scorer. Now, defensive chores apart, his first

*proper touch of the ball was more or less on the hour. He kicked for touch – he had
no choice. Somehow it was a fitting epitaph.*

ENGLAND
J. M. WEBB
R. UNDERWOOD   W. D. C.   CARLING (*capt.*)   J. C. GUSCOTT C.   OTI
R. ANDREW   R. J. HILL
J. LEONARD   B. C. MOORE   J. A. PROBYN
P. J. ACKFORD   W. A. DOOLEY
M. C. TEAGUE   P. J. WINTERBOTTOM   D. RICHARDS

Penalty goals: Webb (3) *Dropped-goal*: Andrew

NEW ZEALAND
T. J. WRIGHT
J. J. KIRWAN   C. R. INNES   B. J. McCAHILL   R. TIMU
G. J. FOX   G. T. M. BACHOP
S. C. McDOWELL   S. B. T. FITZGERALD   R. W. LOE
I. D. JONES   G. W. WHETTON (*capt.*)
A. J. WHETTON   M. N. JONES   Z. V. BROOKE

Replacement: A. Earl for Brooke, 70 minutes
Try: M. N. Jones *Conversion*: Fox *Penalty goals*: Fox (4)

Referee: J. M. Fleming (Scotland)

Breakdown of play (England first)
Scrums with head: 2–16 Scrums against head: 0–0
Line-outs with throw: 13–7 Line-outs against throw: 6–4
Decisive rucks: 20–19 Decisive mauls: 8–3

Michael Jones, scorer of the game's only try, was the first player to score a try
(also from an inside pass) in the 1987 World Cup finals.

Two days later Italy easily beat the United States 30–9 at Otley, to lie second
to New Zealand in England's group, Pool One. By the time England next
took the field, on 8 October, New Zealand had made sure of their quarter-final
place by inflicting an even greater defeat on the Americans, 46–6.

That match began at one o'clock; at three, England were at Twickenham
again, to take on Italy. The only change made by England was enforced by
a knee injury to Wade Dooley, who was replaced by Nigel Redman, the Bath
lock, whose first appearance for England was in 1984, and who also figured
in the inaugural World Cup. Geoff Cooke had hoped to field the same XV
that lost to the All Blacks. England policy on team selection had become, like
many other facets of rugby organisation, much more hard-nosed, and he had
made it clear to the 26-strong national squad that some of them might not
get a match. There was no thought of giving patient reserves a run. Yet John
Mason suggested that since the logical conclusion to this policy meant that,
barring injuries, the first-choice players would play six internationals in 30
days, Mick Skinner and Gary Rees deserved an outing. But the replacements

168

UNDERWOOD BEATS ITALY'S FULL-BACK TROIANI TO SCORE ENGLAND'S FIRST TRY OF THE
WORLD CUP

for the match against Italy were unchanged – D. Pears, S. Halliday, D. Morris,
P. Rendall, J. Olver and M. Skinner – and in the event, one of them did get
on to the field . . .

WEBB WRAPS IT UP

JOHN MASON

*What should have been a salute to full-back Jonathan Webb, whose 24 points against
Italy at Twickenham set an England record, turned into a bitter slanging match, the
first row of the 1991 World Cup. Dean Richards, England's number 8, accused Italy
of cheating and Gianni Zanon, Italy's captain, said he was angry – in translation
the word used was 'sad' – that such charges should have even been hinted at, let
alone made.*

*Scotland's Brian Anderson, the referee, attempted to pour oil on troubled waters
by declaring that none of the 37 penalties he awarded against Italy was for foul play.
However, he was moved to say: 'I did consider sending off an Italian player for
persistent infringement. Certainly I have never awarded so many penalties against
one team in the whole of my refereeing career at any level. When I thought about the
ramifications of a sending-off I thought that it would not help what was becoming a
farcical situation. It could have inflamed the whole match.'*

*In any event, wrong as Richards was to make such provocative remarks – assuming
a private conversation in the Rose Room after the match was correctly reported – it*

169

was difficult to be enthusiastic about a match in which the penalty count (37–10) exceeded the aggregate points (36–6). Judged by that context, England's victory by four goals and four penalty goals was not quite what it appeared, though the stop-start nature of the proceedings made continuity a rare blessing. Anderson went beyond the call of duty at times, in vain, or misunderstood, attempts to prevent Italy from infringing. His efforts deserved a better fate – either that or something has been lost in the Italian translation of Rugby Union's complicated laws. Despite beating the United States at Otley, where Ireland's Owen Doyle was referee, Italy began the match with the biggest penalty count against (18), so suggestions that the Home Unions are conducting some sort of vendetta can be discounted. The Italians, who defended courageously and still sought, legally, to break England's hold when 30 points adrift, would be better advised to acknowledge rugby's laws. They possess the talent, notably Marcello Cuttitta, scrum-half Francescato and Dominguez. Otherwise, omerta (silence) would make more sense.

In some respects England went well. Carling looked more his old self, the strength of his half-breaks in midfield often launching the line, Winterbottom ranged the field hungrily too, and at close quarters Teague demonstrated that he is a hard man either to halt or dispossess. But in the catalogue of excellence, bearing in mind the likely challenge of France in Paris at quarter-final time, the sustained sharpness of Guscott and Webb topped the list by a measure even greater than the penalty count.

England, who in the second half three times accepted the option of scrums instead of penalties, were six points up after the fourth penalty. Territorial possession exceeded 75 per cent and, though there were two more Webb penalty goals, there were also tries for Underwood and Guscott before half-time. Hill hurried round the short side before sending Underwood, who was moved back to the left wing in a pre-match switch, away for his 29th England try. Webb converted from the left-hand touch to hammer home the advantage. Guscott's try, plus conversion, made it 24–0 at the break, the score stemming from a rare Italy attack which went wrong. Andrew set Carling on the move and the early tackles were imperiously brushed aside. Guscott kept him company and, when Troiani moved in for the tackle, Guscott finished behind the posts.

Guscott's second try must be screened for many a day. Webb opened up from the back, Andrew presented the long, long pass and Guscott, from 40 yards out, went on running, rounding the last defender with something to spare. Webb's try came from the umpteenth penalty – a tapped kick by Hill leading to Redman making ground before Guscott, returning the compliment, put Webb in for his first England try. Left-wing Marcello Cuttitta completed what a ricochet and Gaetaniello's swift reactions had started for Italy's try. It was a tiny example of what they might have achieved but for a total disregard for the laws. Referee Anderson, and England, were most patient.

The match involved England's first personnel change – after 53 minutes Paul Rendall replaced his Askean colleague Jeff Probyn, who sustained a strained knee ligament.

ENGLAND

J. M. WEBB

C. OTI   W. D. C. CARLING (*capt.*)   J. C. GUSCOTT   R. UNDERWOOD

C. R. ANDREW   R. J. HILL

J. LEONARD   B. C. MOORE   J. A. PROBYN

P. J. ACKFORD   N. C. REDMAN

M. C. TEAGUE   P. J. WINTERBOTTOM   D. RICHARDS

Replacement: P. A. G. Rendall for Probyn, 53 minutes
Tries: Underwood, Guscott (2), Webb *Conversions*: Webb (4)
Penalty goals: Webb (4)

ITALY
L. TROIANI
P. VACCARI   F. GAETANIELLO   S. BARBA   MARCELLO CUTTITTA
D. DOMINGUEZ   I. FRANCESCATO
MASSIMO CUTTITTA   G. PIVETTA   F. PORPERZI CURTI
R. FAVORO   C. CROCI
R. SAETTI   M. GIOVANELLI   G. ZANON (*capt.*)

Replacement: M. Bonomi for Troiani, 48 minutes
Try: Marcello Cuttitta *Conversion*: Dominguez

Referee: B. Anderson (Scotland)

Breakdown of play (England first)
Scrums with head: 23–7 Scrums against head: 0–0
Line-outs with throw: 10–6 Line-outs against throw: 5–3
Decisive rucks: 20–11 Decisive mauls: 12–3

England's selection against the Eagles, who had conceded 76 points in their previous two matches, was difficult in terms of finding a balance between the first-choice team's overall needs and those of the players who had been kept on the side-lines. It had been decided to keep England's key decision-makers in place. 'These are our people who direct the tactics of the team,' the manager explained.

Underlying this general statement of selectorial principle was the $64,000 question on the immediate playing future of Dean Richards, the number 8 whose drive, power and presence in the first two Cup matches had not been a patch on that of previous seasons, while another player under threat was Chris Oti, who had done wonders to get back on his feet after a long and painful series of knee operations. That last bout had left him a shade off the pace, and Nigel Heslop had taken his place against the United States. Future options might also concern another player returning after a saga of injury – Simon Halliday . . . a possible partner for Carling if Guscott were to revert to his original place in senior rugby, on the wing.

England's XV against the United States eventually made room for seven members of the squad who had not previously played. Heslop and Halliday apart, Hodgkinson returned, with Olver, Skinner, Rees and Pearce, who thus became England's longest-serving international – his career extending to 12 years and 250 days, 160 days longer than that of Jack Heaton in the '30s and '40s. Meanwhile, reserve half-backs Pears and Morris were again assigned to the bench as Carling, Underwood, Andrew, Hill, loosehead Leonard and Richards lined up for their third match in eight days . . . Carling setting a record by leading England for the 22nd time – one more than Bill Beaumont between 1978 and 1982. The final change came with the return of Dooley,

REFEREE PEARD IS ON THE SPOT TO SIGNAL SKINNER'S TRY AGAINST THE USA

who had missed the Italy match through straining a knee in practice at Basingstoke.

THE FRENCH REJECTION

JOHN MASON

Pierre Berbizier, the former France captain and scrum-half, delicately raised a Gallic eyebrow in something less than appreciation of England's third and final pool offering at Twickenham. He was not alone. England, despite a distinct two-fold advantage in possession and territory and a 3–1 bonus in penalty awards, had huffed and puffed their way to an unremarkable victory, in World Cup terms, over the United States.

As some consolation for the home team, who flew to Jersey after the match for an away-from-it-all weekend break, thank goodness for roving Rory Underwood who went looking for work. He scored tries one and five to take his international total to 31 – substantial planks in a 37–9 victory, with four goals, a try and three penalty goals to a goal and a penalty goal.

Applause too for the masterly Dean Richards, the number 8 who ensured that those seeking his replacement in the first-choice team had to eat such unwise words. England would now be sure to play him against France in the quarter-final eight days hence. Even allowing for the suet pudding of a match in which the home team were either ponderous or inefficient, Richards edged towards something approaching known form.

Against fierce-tackling opponents, led inspiringly by the mighty lock Kevin Swords,

172

the sustained examples set by Richards and the combative scrum-half Richard Hill laid the essential foundations of victory. Whether try-scorer Nigel Heslop, the right-wing, did enough to regain the place he filled adequately throughout the Grand Slam of the previous winter would remain a matter for management. Should the opportunity arise, a fit Chris Oti in powerful stride would create a greater threat to the French at close quarters, but changing winning teams is the art of successful selection and England are fortunate to possess this comparative embarrassment of riches.

Much the same could be applied to the full-backs where Hodgkinson, on duty again for the first time since the Grand Slam decider with France at Twickenham, reminded everyone that he is not exactly a liability at this level. He finished with 17 points, made up of four conversions and three penalty goals, to take his points total to 203 in 14 matches. [Only Grant Fox of New Zealand took fewer matches (13 Tests) to achieve a double-century.]

Hodgkinson got matters rolling with a penalty goal (for a ruck offence) in the fifth minute. He followed this with penalty goals in the 12th and 25th minutes and, less a miss in the 52nd minute, was confined to conversion kicks thereafter. Underwood's first try, beginning with Andrew, came after the left-wing had chased a kick ahead by Hodgkinson. Williams, the Eagles centre, looked to have it covered but overran it as Underwood arrived at speed.

Williams, once of Middlesex, Wasps and Metropolitan Police, felt a little better when kicking a penalty goal after 20 minutes, and he also made the important break for the United States try which was scored by full-back Nelson, a one-time Scotland Schools cap.

England's other first-half try-scorer was Carling, who roared through the midfield after Andrew, Halliday, as the pivot, and Underwood, on the burst, had soared beyond the advantage line. Carling carried on at speed, helped on his way by the timing of Halliday's pass. Heslop swept through crowded spaces for his try after Hill and Halliday had created the breach, and the fifth try, in injury time, went to Underwood, lurking this time on the right, who pursued another chip ahead by Hodgkinson after Andrew had launched the raid. Good enough to beat France? Berbizier's enigmatic answer was: 'Peut-être.' . . . He was, I think, being kind.

ENGLAND
S. HODGKINSON
N. HESLOP   W. D. C. CARLING   S. HALLIDAY   R. UNDERWOOD
C. R. ANDREW   R. J. HILL
J. LEONARD   J. OLVER   G. PEARCE
W. A. DOOLEY   N. C. REDMAN
M. SKINNER   G. REES   D. RICHARDS

Tries: Underwood (2), Carling, Skinner, Heslop
Conversions: Hodgkinson (4) *Penalty goals:* Hodgkinson (3)

UNITED STATES
R. NELSON
G. HEIN   M. WILLIAMS   K. HIGGINS   P. SHEEHY
C. O'BRIEN   M. PIDCOCK
L. MANGA   A. FLAY   N. MOTTRAM
C. TUNNACLIFFE   K. SWORDS (*capt.*)
S. LIPMAN   R. FARLEY   A. RIDNELL

Replacements: M. De Jong for Higgins, 40 minutes; J. Wilkerson for Farley, 76 minutes
Try: Nelson *Conversion*: Williams *Penalty goal*: Williams

Referee: L. Peard (Wales)

Breakdown of play (England first)
Scrums with head: 15–12 Scrums without head: 0–0
Line-outs with throw: 11–8 Line-outs against throw: 2–0
Decisive rucks won: 22–5 Decisive mauls won: 6–4

POOL RESULTS AND STANDINGS

POOL ONE

	P	W	D	L	F	A	Pts
NEW ZEALAND	3	3	0	0	95	39	9
ENGLAND	3	2	0	1	85	33	7
ITALY	3	1	0	2	57	76	5
US	3	0	0	3	24	113	3

Results: England 12 – New Zealand 18; Italy 30 – United States 9; New Zealand 46 – United States 6; England 36 – Italy 6; England 37 – United States 9; New Zealand 31 – Italy 21

POOL TWO

	P	W	D	L	F	A	Pts
SCOTLAND	3	3	0	0	122	36	9
IRELAND	3	2	0	1	102	51	7
JAPAN	3	1	0	2	77	87	5
ZIMBABWE	3	0	0	3	31	158	3

Results: Scotland 47 – Japan 9, Ireland 55 – Zimbabwe 11; Scotland 51 – Zimbabwe 12; Ireland 32 – Japan 16; Scotland 24 – Ireland 15; Japan 52 – Zimbabwe 8

POOL THREE

	P	W	D	L	F	A	Pts
AUSTRALIA	3	3	0	0	79	25	9
W. SAMOA	3	2	0	1	54	34	7
WALES	3	1	0	2	32	61	5
ARGENTINA	3	0	0	3	38	83	3

Results: Australia 32 – Argentina 19; Wales 13 – Western Samoa 16; Australia 9 – Western Samoa 3; Wales 16 – Argentina 7; Wales 3 – Australia 38; Argentina 12 – Western Samoa 35

POOL FOUR

	P	W	D	L	F	A	Pts
FRANCE	3	3	0	0	82	25	9
CANADA	3	2	0	1	45	33	7
ROMANIA	3	1	0	2	31	64	5
FIJI	3	0	0	3	27	63	3

Results: France 30 – Romania 3; Fiji 3 – Canada 13; France 33 – Fiji 9; Canada 19 – Romania 11; Fiji 15 – Romania 17; France 19 – Canada 13

Prophesying the exact final order in England's group, and that of Scotland, would not have taxed many rugby aficionados. Western Samoa upset Wales from Pool Three with a forthright display at Cardiff, though the Welsh case was not helped by the fact that the French referee was unsighted when Robert Jones got his hand to a ball behind the Welsh try-line and not, as the referee ruled, a West Samoan – whose team thus proved that the times they are a-changing and qualified for the quarter-final against Scotland at Murrayfield. Australia's next stop was Dublin, where the Irish awaited them and where New Zealand, due to meet Canada at Lille, could confidently expect to meet the Wallabies for a place in the final. England got on with their Jersey weekend away from it all, and the tide of hype rose inexorably . . . as did the number of column inches, in the popular press as well now, on England's chances of wrestling a semi-final place from France in Paris.

There was some rough stuff as England began full training at the Montmorency Club, north-east of the capital. Physical contact was never shirked, and several players required treatment; an exchange between Richards and Moore was not confined to mere words. The next day – with 24 hours to go before the quarter-final the most significant selection decision in years put Richards on the Parc des Princes replacements bench. The back-row permutations of the build-up games had borne a bitter fruit for the Leicester number 8, so long a sturdy fixture in the England plans. Skinner, Winterbottom and Teague were to be the new pattern of things, while Heslop came in for Oti.

These were unforced changes: France were less fortunate, since Didier Camberabero's damaged ribs led the team doctor to rule him out for the match. The outside-half had wanted to play with his ribs strapped, but fresh X-ray pictures showed that this would be unwise, so Thierry Lacroix took his place. Philippe Sella convinced the management that his thigh strain was

BLANCO WITH GUSCOTT IN CLOSE ATTENDANCE

no problem, and Saint-André moved to the other wing. He had scored against Wales and England last season when, he said: 'I really had the feeling I was playing with the best three-quarter line in the world.'

Meanwhile Scotland found that their Western Samoan opponents in the Murrayfield quarter-final would not include Ma'taafa Keenan, whose appeal against suspension was rejected. He had been sent off for fighting at Pontypridd the previous Sunday, along with Pedro Sporleder of Argentina. By the day of the match, Craig Chalmers had been passed fit for the Scots. However, Sean Lineen, their New Zealand-born inside-centre, had to be replaced by Graham Shiel, who had been put on instead of Chalmers – and scored – in his début against Ireland in the final pool match, won 24–15 to complete a 100 per cent record. Scotland found few problems in qualifying (28–6) to meet the winners of France v England either, and, as the Murrayfield match began two hours before the one in Paris, England took the field there knowing that victory would give them a chance to revenge the Grand Slam defeat suffered in 1990 at the Scottish HQ. Torrents of words and countless gallons of printers' ink were lavished on how England overcame the

French, but not nearly as many as were needed in the days that followed to plot the course of events derived from incidents in the players' tunnel soon after the match.

PARC DE TRIOMPHE   JOHN MASON

Victory was everything in England's quarter-final at Parc des Princes, and not even lurid tales of assaults on referee David Bishop of New Zealand as the teams left the field could spoil England's moments of triumph. Whatever reservations there might be about the way in which it was done, the incontrovertible fact was that resolute, single-minded England beat nervy, inefficient France on every count.

The reward for successfully playing the percentages, as well as recognising scoring opportunities, was a World Cup semi-final at Murrayfield with Scotland. For France, at odds with themselves let alone England, there was little but disarray, dissension and, for coach Daniel Dubroca and prop Pascal Ondarts, disgrace.

Nor did Serge Blanco, a pale, irritable imitation of a marvellous gifted player, endear himself in what was presumed to be his farewell match. Either the occasion or the cares of office got to him because, sad to relate, Blanco's short-comings helped to establish the foundations for England's rough-hewn victory by a goal, a try and three penalty goals to a try and two penalty goals – 19–10.

England, understandably, were well pleased with themselves. The forwards cleared the trail, captain Carling had an outstanding match in every respect and, with a touch of class at the precise moment from Guscott, England had won a prize which I, for one, believed to be beyond their reach. Skinner, who should have a gold medal for one tackle alone on Cecillon, did exactly as the selectors required in his roving blind-side flank role and, in the last quarter, Ackford ruled the line-out in a way which must have set the alarms ringing north of the Border. Whether the decision to drop Richards and move Teague to number 8 was justified would remain as debatable as it was beforehand. One bonus, at least, was that a selection fraught with pros and cons did not rebound to England's detriment. The same arguments would recur in committee, though Skinner's Richter-scale work had to secure his place, barring injury, and the main area of contention would be restricted to whether Teague should remain at number 8 to the continuing exclusion of Richards. Manager Geoff Cooke could not resist a dig – ridiculous was the word he used – at the team's critics, conveniently forgetting that he too had spoken less than enthusiastically about England's performances in recent months. It is right and proper that mother hen should bridle.

The tattoo that French fists beat on Heslop's chin in the opening minutes after he had pursued his own high kick set unenviable standards. Blanco, piqued at being challenged after calling a mark, joined in vigorously after Champ had let fly. The Bishop lectures began early. That was penalty goal number one to Webb and, when another short-arm came piling in on Teague three minutes later, England were six points up and France had scarcely set foot outside their territory.

The extremely bothered Lacroix, after dropping the ball initially, was in much better heart after kicking a penalty goal when England were off-side. Flanker Cabannes had a strong influence on the proceedings that followed, though it was England who stated the next definitive case with a fine try. England won a two-man line-out and with the ball being quickly worked to the left, Carling timed his pass acutely. Guscott straightened, showed Blanco the ball and shuffled, at speed, either way. In the last stride, Guscott decided not to take on the full-back and unleashed the ball to Underwood for the try – a flat, sharp pass that some of the opposition claimed was forward. I doubt it.

Lacroix's second penalty goal – off-side again – took the score to 6–10 at half-time, and 11 minutes into the second half Lafond scored the try that gave France hope. It stemmed from a free-kick, the ball rebounding off Webb's shoulder. Galthié kept moving to his left and, though almost running out of space, was able to present Lafond with the scoring pass. The score was locked at 10–10 for 24 minutes, and with extra-time looming fast, Webb's third penalty goal crept over the bar after Ondarts, to his fury, had been penalised for seeking the ball illegally. He was not happy, especially after England had offered him a few words, none of them consoling.

With Ackford in command of his kingdom in the final minutes, England were safe. Hill made quite sure with another high, hanging kick. Lafond was beneath the ball and, for his pains, was driven over the line. Carling, as ever, was first up and his try, converted by Webb, was entirely appropriate.

FRANCE
S. BLANCO (*capt.*)
J.-B. LAFOND   P. SELLA   F. MESNEL   P. SAINT-ANDRÉ
T. LACROIX   F. GALTHIÉ
G. LASCUBE   P. MAROCCO   P. ONDARTS
J.-M. CADIEU   O. ROUMAT
E. CHAMP   L. CABANNES   M. CECILLON

Try: Lafond *Penalty goals*: Lacroix (2)

ENGLAND
J. M. WEBB
N. HESLOP   W. D. C. CARLING (*capt.*)   J. C. GUSCOTT   R. UNDERWOOD
C. R. ANDREW   R. J. HILL
J. LEONARD   B. C. MOORE   J. A. PROBYN
P. J. ACKFORD   W. A. DOOLEY
M. SKINNER   P. J. WINTERBOTTOM   M. C. TEAGUE

Tries: Underwood, Carling *Conversion*: Webb *Penalty goals*: Webb (3)

Referee: D. Bishop (New Zealand)

Breakdown of play (England first)
Scrums with head: 22–16 Scrums against head: 1–0
Line-outs with throw: 17–7 Line-outs against throw: 4–1
Decisive rucks won: 13–14 Decisive mauls won: 3–7
Overall percentage possession: 57–43

Carling's try was the fifth of his Test career and his third against France. He scored at Twickenham in 1989 and in Paris in 1990.

The length of time taken by the organising committee and the French authorities to react to what happened in the tunnel was viewed, justifiably, by many observers, as bringing rugby into disrepute even more than the original transgressions. There can be little doubt about what did occur. Eye witnesses in the tunnel said that Pascal, the French tighthead prop, tried to chase David Bishop, the referee, to his dressing-room. Jeff Herdman, a former Swansea player and a member of the Barbarians committee, was among those present, in his role as a BBC Radio Wales commentator. He described a further incident, involving the French coach, Daniel Dubroca: 'I know what I saw and have broadcast that. I was waiting in the tunnel to conduct post-match interviews and everything happened within feet of where I was standing. I saw Dubroca pin the referee, David Bishop, by the lapels of his jersey and scream repeatedly in English one word only: "Cheat!"'

'I know nothing about any spitting and nor did a French player strike the referee. Dubroca was pulled away from Bishop and after that there were other scuffles, none of which involved anyone in authority.'

Dubroca's version of this was that he had thanked the referee for the match, and offered him fraternal greetings. Since Ondarts appeared to take a swing at Bishop during the match, mercifully missing, fraternity was one of the Revolutionary watch-words not in general use at the Parc that day.

The affair could not rest there. Within 48 hours, Roger Quittenton, the last of whose 18 international matches as referee was in 1989, was demanding a full inquiry. By the time 72 hours had passed, Dubroca was writing a letter of apology to the French Rugby Federation president Albert Ferrasse. But still the controversy raged on, since Ray Williams, the tournament director, ruled out action by the World Cup committee. He said: 'Our tournament chairman Russell Thomas has discussed the matter with Albert Ferrasse, who says Dubroca wrote that he bitterly regrets the incident and says he never intended to question the honesty of David Bishop. Dubroca's words indicate he used the word cheat and now regrets it. We must rely on the good sense of the French Federation to deal with the matter properly.'

Good sense seemed to be at a premium in the game's hierarchy. Among those who called the authorities to order was H. J. Heinz, not only backers of a series of fair play awards, but the first major sponsors of the 1991 Cup. Bruce Purgavie, deputy managing director of Heinz UK, pointed out the futility of trying to sweep the affair under the carpet. 'We are not happy about it . . . we have made our point of view known. No doubt it is being listened to.' No doubt it was, since Heinz had put up £800,000 for the privilege of being associated with rugby at the top level and Purgavie put Heinz's attitude in a nutshell with: 'We do not want to be sullied in any way.'

Ray Williams stuck to the point that the referee had not made a formal complaint in his report. But since by the fifth day after the incident Dubroca was declaring he had no plans to resign, Williams was instructed to write to Ferrasse to reopen the issue – for now the referee had confirmed, in his official report, counter-signed by his Irish and New Zealand touch-judges, that 'a serious incident' had occurred in the Parc tunnel.

Next day, on the eve of the Scotland-England semi-final, Dubroca resigned, and Russell Thomas, chairman of the Rugby World Cup 1991 accepted that he had been wrong on the morrow of the match not to take further action. Once the official complaint had been received, it had been inevitable that

Dubroca would go, but Ferrasse was still criticising the RWC for changing their minds after the coach's initial apology: 'It's not the first time. The English are not made like others. There is not a single French referee in the World Cup. Are our referees also lepers?' Dubroca accused 'the British' of using the referee's report 'to destabilise French rugby'. *L'Equipe*, the French sports daily which had tried to inspire the French team by asking them to *'Imaginez l'horreur'* of losing to England in the Parc, put the Dubroca case differently: 'His gesture,' the paper said, 'condemns French rugby even more than Rob Andrew's up-and-unders.'

Meanwhile, the queues for Scotland-England tickets snaked back from the Murrayfield sales points, and Dublin licked its lips at the prospect of New Zealand, easy victors (29–13) over Canada at Lille, v Australia, who had scraped a 19–18 win over Ireland at Lansdowne Road.

England's only change for the most important of their meetings with Scotland in 120 years was Simon Halliday for Nigel Heslop, who had been unable to remember much of the Parc des Princes set-to after his run in with Blanco and Co. Scotland had Sean Lineen back after injury. If any additional motivation were needed by England, their manager Geoff Cooke provided it with the subtle point that failure to beat Scotland would mean three days in Cardiff the following week for the third-place play-off.

BULLDOZER CHARIOT

JOHN MASON

England, impervious to the slings and arrows, remorsely exploited every known game plan from A to B to secure victory over Scotland and a place in the World Cup final at Twickenham. As an exercise in the rigid adherence to one tactical scheme, muscular England, who won by two penalty goals and a dropped-goal to two penalty goals, barely put a foot wrong. Feet were the feat.

Scotland, squeezed in the scrum, stretched in the line-out, were left with crumbs, desperately trying to keep the game alive. Permitted the ball only on England's terms, they struggled. The forwards, ultimately, were obliterated. If the valiant back row of Finlay Calder, John Jeffrey and Derek White, who have served Scotland mightily through the years, did not have a happy afternoon, their front five colleagues fared even worse, notably David Sole, the captain, on the loose-head.

In what turned out to be their last international appearance at Murrayfield, Jeffrey, who led the team out, and company also met their final match in Mick Skinner, Peter Winterbottom and Mike Teague, ironically the England back row who had faltered in the 1990 Grand Slam match on the same ground. But England, drawing increasing strength from the line-out domination of Ackford and Dooley and the pin-point kicking of Andrew, could not create a celebration try for Underwood in his 50th international. None of the England team, though, will have been complaining.

Scotland led from the eighth minute to the 57th. It was another 16 minutes after that before England went ahead for the first time. To have run the auld enemy so close for so long was, in the event, an achievement of consequence against the odds. The knowledge will have been of no comfort whatsoever.

I once wrote of a dreadful performance by Richmond – which, as a new venture at the time, was being video-taped for coaching purposes – that the players should

180

ARMSTRONG GIVES ACKFORD THE SORT OF LIFT HE DOESN'T NEED, HELPED BY JEFFREY
(FACING THE CAMERA)

be taken to a desert island and made to watch the tape twice a day from Monday to Saturday and four times on Sunday. They should invite England as their guests. Now I accept that there was nothing dreadful about efficient England's systematic destruction of Scotland's pack – only a fearful inevitability, the grim rattle of the tumbrils of defeat through Edinburgh's grey, damp cobbled streets. What was galling, though – the yawn of the tournament, the flat denial of all-round skills – was the near wilful refusal to admit that the match might be played in another way, given the flood of English possession. It will be argued that the four penalty goal misses by Webb in the third, 15th, 49th and 51st minutes left England without a cushion, without the safety net of points required to guarantee an appearance in the final against Australia at Twickenham seven days hence rather than Cardiff for the third-place play-off.

Webb was not alone in falling prey to frayed nerves and, indeed, allowed himself the faintest of smiles over (relatively) straightforward goals for collapsed scrums in the 32nd and 57th minutes to lift England from 0–6, to 3–6 to 6–6 and everything to play for with, give or take time added for injury and stoppages, 23 minutes remaining. But Gavin Hastings, who for more than an hour had looked to be inhabiting the levels reserved only for the superstars, hit the wall of harsh reality scarcely four minutes after Webb's second penalty goal had levelled the score.

Unwisely, Skinner, whose tackle on Cecillon in Paris the previous week was a marvellous moment of controlled aggression, suddenly lost his temper. Two wrongs do not make a right and with referee Kerry Fitzgerald completely and commendably in charge, England were penalised slightly to Scotland's right of the posts. Grim-faced England stolidly faced the kicker, the lead about to be frittered away. Up dashed Hastings and the ball, struck hard, flew high to the right of the posts – a straight trajectory instead of the slight angle the kicker had intended as a matter of course. That was in the 61st minute and England, the reprieve granted, could not be moved thereafter.

The vice tightened and tightened. There was a glorious, ghosting, swerving run by Underwood, put away by Moore, in no space at all on the left. At the last stride, the try-line beckoning, Gaving Hastings, with Calder as back-up, got his man. The ball was tossed back as the tackle came and Moore, arms outstretched, was within an ace of taking the ball until a Scotland body deflected it. But the territory had been won and England, pawing the ground in their anxiety to pile-drive through a weary mass of blue jerseys, had old scores, labelled March 1990, to repay.

Six times that scrum packed down in England's left-hand attacking corner. It went to the floor twice, it swivelled round, Teague was held, it crabbed nearer the posts and swivelled again. The sixth time, on Carling's instruction, the ball was released, Hill to Andrew, Scotland on their knees. Half a pace, steady and a drop for goal by Andrew, right-footed from an angle on the left. As the ball climbed between the posts, the clock said 3.51 p.m. and England were homeward bound, this time to Twickenham. Unlike in 1990, it was the blue jerseys who had tae think again: the flowers of Scotland had wilted.

SCOTLAND
A. G. HASTINGS
A. G. STANGER   S. HASTINGS   S. R. P. LINEEN   I. TUKALO
C. M. CHALMERS   G. ARMSTRONG
D. M. B. SOLE (*capt.*)   J. ALLAN   A.P. BURNELL
C. A. GRAY   G. W. WEIR
J. JEFFREY   F. CALDER   D. B. WHITE

Penalty goals: G. Hastings (2)

ENGLAND
J. M. WEBB
S. HALLIDAY   W. D. C. CARLING (*capt.*)   J. C. GUSCOTT   R. UNDERWOOD
C. R. ANDREW   R. J. HILL
J. LEONARD   B. C. MOORE   J. A. PROBYN
P. J. ACKFORD   W. A. DOOLEY
M. G. SKINNER   P. J. WINTERBOTTOM   M. C. TEAGUE

Penalty goals: Webb (2) *Dropped-goal*: Andrew

Referee: K. V. J. Fitzgerald (Australia)

Breakdown of play (England first)
Scrums with head: 18–18 Scrums against head: 0–0
Line-outs with throw: 14–14 Line-outs against throw: 6–1
Decisive rucks: 14–15 Decisive mauls: 7–1
Overall percentage of possession: 55–45

The match was the second of the 1991 World Cup devoid of tries, the first being when Australia beat Western Samoa in heavy rain at Pontypool. Tries were scored in all the 1987 Cup matches.

182

Andrew's dropped-goal, his 15th, equalled the records for senior international board countries set by J.-P. Lescarboura (France) and Naas Botha (South Africa).

England's win elicited widely conflicting views. Ian McGeechan, Scotland' coach, charged that 'They were going to strangle the game and we were trying to keep it alive.' Carling pointed out that Scotland had been unbeaten in 13 home matches (since McGeechan took over for the defeat against Australia in 1988). Moore looked forward: 'We believe our Twickenham factor will be better for us than Scotland's Murrayfield factor was for them.' But the bookies at once made Australia, 16–6 winners over New Zealand the day after Scotland were eliminated, favourites for the Cup. Campese made one try and scored another, while Grant Fox had not so much as a shot at goal in the first half. In the second, Australia proved just as solid in defence as sharp in attack, and their line remained inviolate, though Fox kicked two penalty goals.

England began their preparations for the final in Grantham, where Margaret Thatcher spent her early years. From there, Carling promised that a different England would be seen in the final. 'We've already accepted we won't win the World Cup playing like we did at Murrayfield.'

Nick Farr-Jones, the Australian captain, took leave to doubt that, when he arrived at Heathrow Airport with four days to go to the final. England, he thought, were entitled to adopt whatever tactics they liked. Bob Dwyer, the Wallaby coach, might well have been playing a deeper word game, one of double-bluff, when he said: 'England would be stupid not to play what they consider to be a winning game. I think they see themselves playing to their big strength, their excellent forwards. There's less margin for error, I suppose. On the other hand, if I find it boring I'm within my rights to say so. That's not a criticism, it's more a statement of how it affects me.' Was Dwyer attempting to 'dare' England into changing their game plan to a pattern which he thought might be more vulnerable to Australian strengths?

Whatever changes might be made in tactics, changes in personnel for the final were there none; both teams were announced as unchanged, including those nominated as replacements. England were forced into a change 48 hours later, with two days left to the final, because Paul Rendall, England's senior prop, had to undergo an immediate operation to an Achilles tendon ruptured during training at the Stoop ground next door to Twickenham. Gary Pearce was named to take his place on the reserves bench.

Attention was diverted from Twickenham considerations for a few hours on the Wednesday night before the final by the third-place play-off at Cardiff, where New Zealand needed all manner of persistence to overcome the Scots 13–6. Walter Little's scything runs constantly threatened to add a try to the usual diet of penalty goals (in the end the tally was three to New Zealand and two to Scotland), and not until the final seconds did the All Blacks manage to get across Scotland's line, Little doing the trick after the ball was moved left, and full-back Terry Wright made the final pass. New Zealand's penalty goals were kicked by Jon Preston, who gained his place in the squad as a utility back, playing in place of the injured Grant Fox at Cardiff . . . where John Jeffrey and Finlay Calder finished their Scotland careers, having caused England a good deal of grief along the way.

So it was time for 'God Save the Queen' (to whom both teams were presented) and 'Advance Australia Fair' (with the aid of song-sheets for most Aussies don't know the words) – and into the second World Cup final. England started with a blustery wind at their backs . . .

CAMPESE TAKES A HAND
JOHN MASON

An off-colour but happy Nick Farr-Jones, captain of the World Cup-winning Wallabies, fiercely defended David Campese's deliberate knock-on of a possible England try-scoring pass with barely ten minutes remaining at Twickenham. Scrum-half Farr-Jones, who had to leave the post-final official dinner early because he was unwell, said he did not believe the incident in the 70th minute of a fascinating, stomach-churning contest warranted a penalty try after Campese, one-handed, had knocked down a pass from Peter Winterbottom to Rory Underwood:

'You don't award a penalty in those situations, but I can understand the English frustrations because this was one of the few times they really looked to have a really good chance of crossing our line. I would have done exactly the same thing as Campo, if I'd been near enough.'

With about ten minutes remaining and the score 12–3 to the Wallabies, Campese, coming infield from the right wing, reached round Winterbottom as the flanker, having received the ball from Will Carling, sought to release an unmarked Underwood on the left. Campese, using his right hand and making no attempt to intercept, knocked the ball down and forward as Winterbottom shaped to pass. Underwood, almost in stride, was left stranded, the ball eluded everyone for a fraction before Campese got to it and referee Bevan, pausing momentarily to see who was where, ran back at a diagonal to award the penalty.

Would Underwood have scored? Bearing in mind that in six World Cup matches, Australia, at that point, had only conceded three tries (two to Argentina and one to Ireland), it would not be wise to be dogmatic, though plainly Campese saw Underwood as an acute threat. Horan, the most complete tackler in the tournament, was going flat out for the south-east touch-line. Lynagh, at the sharper angle, was scooting towards the corner flag and Farr-Jones was also making hurried tracks midway between the two. Horan might have nailed Underwood but I doubt that the other two would have cut him off. Who knows?

Though full-back Jonathan Webb kicked the goal, England were seething, especially Brian Moore, the hooker and pack leader, who is rarely given to charitable thoughts about opponents – of any nationality. Moore thundered: 'Campese has gone through this tournament telling everyone how he's the saviour of rugby. But he proved that he's as cynical as the rest of us when it comes down to it. He's a brilliant player but let's hear the last of him being some kind of saint.'

That such passions should have been roused should surprise no one. The struggle for the Webb Ellis Trophy, the prize for Rugby Union World Champions, which Australia won by a goal and two penalty goals to two penalty goals, brought a match

CARLING WATCHES LYNAGH SCORE
WITH A PENALTY

of such intensity that in a lifetime of playing, watching, refereeing and watching, I would be hard-pressed to name a comparable occasion.

I will risk the sceptical groan by suggesting that considering what was at stake rugby was the winner. Here was a match of spell-binding authority, bravery, and, believe it or not, goodwill. England, the losers, saved their best until last and if it is felt that some of their ringcraft was a fraction below par because of prior neglect, I doubt very much whether the Australians would agree. Yet their victory was scarcely in the style for which, rightly, Australia have become renowned – ball in hand, rapid second- or third-phase possession and support ranging left, right and down the middle. They also lost out at the line-out, frequently incurring stricture from referee Bevan. The brakes came on early, applied with maximum efficiency by England, who reminded the world that they did know a thing or two about back play. The demands, accentuated by the commanding presence of Teague, Skinner and Winterbottom, the massive bulldogs in the back-row, left Australia with a host of problems.

It is infinitely to the credit of Poidevin, the flanker, of Horan and Little in the centre, and of outside-half Lynagh for his controlled kicking in a tricky wind, that a golden defensive wall could not be scaled at any stage. Here were the major aspects of the New Zealand semi-final the previous Sunday all over again. In the midst of these defensive chores – a stunning tackle by Eales, the lock, on the alert Andrew and another by Egerton, the left wing, on Halliday were further examples of the total commitment fore and aft – Australia maintained an enviable calm. They possessed the composure, the time, the vision to search for gaps and opportunities to force England on to the back foot.

It was Horan who finally pinned England down after the immaculate Lynagh had kicked a penalty goal in the 27th minute to give the Wallabies the lead – a

185

Dooley line-out offence. Busy Andrew, who made 26 passes from outside-half and kicked only 14 times, chipped deep for Underwood on the left, the ball not having previously reached the wing without the odd mishap, be it overrunning, poor pass, or shattering tackle. Horan was there waiting, judging his moment superbly. There was a glimmer of space on the north-west touch and away Horan went at speed. The counter left England's players slamming into reverse gear and, although the cover converged, some 70 metres had been re-won before the ball could be scrambled to touch, deep in England's half, this time on the south-west touch.

At the line-out, a barn door masquerading as Ofahengaue reached for the ball. Instantly, he was flanked left, right and behind. The maul crabbed rapidly to England's line and, with a fearful inevitability, sank to the earth, the ball, magnet-like, in the clutch of the props, Daly and McKenzie. White-jerseyed arms could do nothing. After much post-match debate, and no little humour, the try was claimed by Daly. Lynagh converted from close to touch and Australia, with half-an-hour gone, were 9–0 up. Webb missed his first two kicks at goal late in the half and though, golf-like, the yips did not persist, the chance to exert pressure on some increasingly tense Wallabies was lost. So, too, were England's backs at times, even though Guscott did set Australian knees knocking in a series of sweeping runs.

All were in vain. England found the tunnel easily enough, but not, alas, the guiding light at the end of it. Webb's penalty goal in the 61st minute (McCall, line-out) had little value in that Lynagh replied in kind seven minutes later when Teague tumbled over the top of a ruck.

The final act involved Campese, after a tapped penalty had set Ackford and Dooley trundling at the core of the Australian pack. Back came the ball sweetly and, with a surge by Skinner and a pick-up and feed by Carling, Webb sent Halliday down the west touch-line. Egerton's tackle could not prevent the ball coming back inside, and again England's line moved menacingly. Teague and Hill pounced and Carling handed on to Winterbottom. For a moment the world stood still. Underwood was in the starting blocks and there was room on the left. In strode Campese and, penalty goal to come or not, as the ball hit the deck so did England's chances of victory.

ENGLAND
J. M. WEBB

S. HALLIDAY   W. D. C. CARLING (*capt.*)   J. C. GUSCOTT   R. UNDERWOOD

C. R. ANDREW   R. J. HILL

J. LEONARD   B. C. MOORE   J. A. PROBYN

P. J. ACKFORD   W. A. DOOLEY

M. G. SKINNER   P. J. WINTERBOTTOM   M. C. TEAGUE

Penalty goals: Webb (2)

AUSTRALIA
ROEBUCK

CAMPESE   LITTLE   HORAN   EGERTON

LYNAGH   FARR-JONES (capt.)

DALY   KEARNS   McKENZIE

McCALL   EALES

POIDEVIN   OFAHENGAUE   COKER

Try: Daly *Conversion*: Lynagh *Penalty goals*: Lynagh (2)

186

WHAT A RELIEF – EALES (IN THE HEAD-BAND) AND DALY REALISE IT'S ALL OVER, 1991 WORLD CUP FINAL

Referee: W. D. Bevan (Wales)

Breakdown of play (England first)
Scrums with head 15–14 Scrums against head: 0–0
Line-outs with throw: 17–15 Line-outs against throw: 9–3
Decisive rucks: 9–34 Decisive mauls: 5–12
Overall percentage possession won: 41–59

Apart from Coker (in Gavin's place at number 8), the Wallaby XV was the same as the one that beat England in July; England personnel changes from that match were Halliday for Oti, Dooley for Bayfield, and Skinner for Richards.

Incidents in the turmoil of Cup-final battle apart, what was the real cause of England defeat? Jamie Salman said it was because England had succumbed to the hype about their playing style and chose this match to enter uncharted waters for the first time in the tournament . . . 'a couple of what the Wallabies call high bombs were very much in order', while Peter FitzSimons put it down to England breaking Dwyer's number-one Cardinal Sin: 'Thou shalt not lose the ball in the tackle.'

Whatever the truth of this, as Australia made off with the Cup, Carling announced that he would have naught to do with League offers, but that another Grand Slam and, in due time, World Cup campaign were his targets. Uttley gave way to Dick Best as coach, and Best and Cooke named their areas of special interest in developing the team for the next (Five Nations) challenge – Best with the forwards, Cooke with the backs. Further, the players were keen to have Cooke confirmed as a full-time functionary. 'It's a full-time job,' said Carling, and who could raise their voice against that judgment?

The changes wrought in the expectations of players and public by the Cup would take time to sink in – but if Carling, Andrew and Hiller were to see their desired reforms put in place, there would have to be a change of heart by at least one administrator, for tournament director Ray Williams, on the morrow of the final, dismissed suggestions that the players involved deserved payment. 'The International Board has laid down the laws on amateurism,' he said. 'They have been accepted by the playing countries in the world . . . I've always said that behind every international player stand a thousand volunteers.' 1991 internationals might ask if all volunteers took five weeks off (a conservative estimate) for the Cup.

The debate will continue, and so will the England planning to go one better next time. 1991 had been, arguably, the best in their history – 12 internationals, half of them away, and only three lost. Crucially for 1995, wherever the Cup might be played, those defeats were by Southern Hemisphere sides. There would doubtless be a third next time – one on each side of the final draw pattern. What chance then of any European side making the final?

The advances made by the supposed minnows of the 1991 Cup suggest

BLOODY, AND WITH THE ENGLAND CAPTAIN ABOUT TO DESCEND ON HIM, ROEBUCK CLEARS, 1991 WORLD CUP FINAL

ACKFORD'S TARGET IS YOUNG WALLABY LOCK EALES, 1991 WORLD CUP FINAL

there may be surprises in store. If the upward curve on the graph of English rugby reformation can be continued, particularly in the sphere of coaching at all levels and marketing and finance generally, England are perfectly capable of providing shocks in any hemisphere.

Many of the fans will forever rue the change of tactics against Australia. Had the management not so ordained, might not Carling's team have emerged as a triumphant 'sweet juggernaut'?

THE CONTRIBUTORS

STEVE BALE	Rugby correspondent of the *Independent*, from Wales
MICHAEL BLAIR	*Birmingham Post* rugby correspondent
HENRI BRU	Editor of rugby coverage of French sports daily, *L'Équipe*
DON CAMERON	*New Zealand Herald* writer for cricket and rugby
TERRY COOPER	Press Association rugby correspondent
BARRIE FAIRALL	Career as prop stunted by demands of writing career, Rosslyn Park member, and editor of *The Year of the Rose: England's Grand Slam '91*
PETER FITZSIMONS	Seven Australian caps as second row and 'hoping for more,' playing three times against England in provincial games in Australia but never in a Test. Lived in France and wrote for English publications
BRENDAN GALLAGHER	London Irish man who worked in South Wales, now a frequent *Telegraph* contributor with Hayter's Sports Services
DAVID GREEN	Oxford cricket Blue, who played for Lancashire and Gloucestershire at cricket, and for Sale and Bristol at rugby: regular cricket and rugby writer for the *Daily Telegraph*
JOHN GRIFFITHS	Schoolmaster and rugby statistician from Wales
BOB HILLER	Harlequin and England captain, and England full-back 1968–72: now a schoolmaster
CHRIS JONES	Respected freelance rugby writer and editor of the *Daily Telegraph Rugby Union World Cup Guide*
WILLIE JOHN McBRIDE	Irish international, and led unbeaten Lions on tour of South Africa in 1974

NORMAN MAIR	Scottish international who played for Edinburgh University. He is golf writer for the *Observer* and writes a rugby column for the *Scotsman*
JOHN MASON	Rugby correspondent of the *Daily Telegraph* since 1979, and staunch West Countryman
TERRY O'CONNOR	Former *Daily Mail* rugby correspondent who played for Saracens
A. C. PARKER	Rugby correspondent and former Sports Editor for the Cape Town *Argus*, covering 12 Springbok tours and author of ten books on Rugby Union
BRIAN PRICE	Almost ever-present for Wales in the '60s – broadcasting summariser
CHRIS REA	Scottish international, played for West of Scotland and Headingley, rugby correspondent of the *Independent on Sunday* and TV commentator
CHARLES RANDALL	*Daily Telegraph* cricket and rugby writer and capable club cricketer
JOHN REASON	Rugby correspondent successively of the *Daily* and *Sunday Telegraph*
GRAHAM TAIT	Former Deputy Sports Editor, *Telegraph* northern edition and now northern rugby correspondent
ROGER UTTLEY	England and Lions forward and director of Harrow School Sports Centre. Only man to play in and then coach a Grand Slam team (ever-present forward in 1980 and coach in 1991). OBE for services to rugby
CHALKIE WHITE	Former Leicester coach, Technical Administrator for the South and South-West
DUDLEY WOOD	Secretary of the Rugby Football Union, and celebrated after-dinner speaker